GRAPHIC HISTORY

THE Pilgrims AND THE First Thanksgiving

by Mary Englar
illustrated by Peter McDonnell

Consultant:

Melodie Andrews, PhD
Associate Professor of Early American History
Minnesota State University, Mankato

Capstone press®

Mankato, Minnesota

Graphic Library is published by Capstone Press,
151 Good Counsel Drive, P.O. Box 669, Mankato, Minnesota 56002.
www.capstonepress.com

Printed in the United States of America

1 2 3 4 5 6 11 10 09 08 07 06

Library of Congress Cataloging-in-Publication Data
Englar, Mary.
The Pilgrims and the first Thanksgiving / by Mary Englar; illustrated by Peter McDonnell
p. cm.—(Graphic library. Graphic history)
Includes bibliographical references and index.
ISBN-13: 978-0-7368-5492-4 (hardcover)
ISBN-10: 0-7368-5492-4 (hardcover)
ISBN-13: 978-0-7368-7529-5 (softcover)
ISBN-10: 0-7368-7529-8 (softcover)
1. Pilgrims (New Plymouth Colony)—Juvenile literature. 2. Massachusetts—History—New Plymouth, 1620-1691—Juvenile literature. 3. Thanksgiving Day—Juvenile literature. I. Title. II. Series.
F68.E55 2007
974.4'02—dc22 2006014724

Summary: In graphic novel format, tells the devastating story of the Pilgrims' first year in America up until their Harvest Festival.

Designer
Jason Knudson

Editor
Mandy Robbins

Editor's note: Direct quotations from primary sources are indicated by a yellow background.

Direct quotations appear on the following pages:
Pages 7, 11, 20, from *Of Plymouth Plantation: 1620–1647* by William Bradford (New York: Random House, 1981).

Table of Contents

Chapter 1
Arriving in the New World

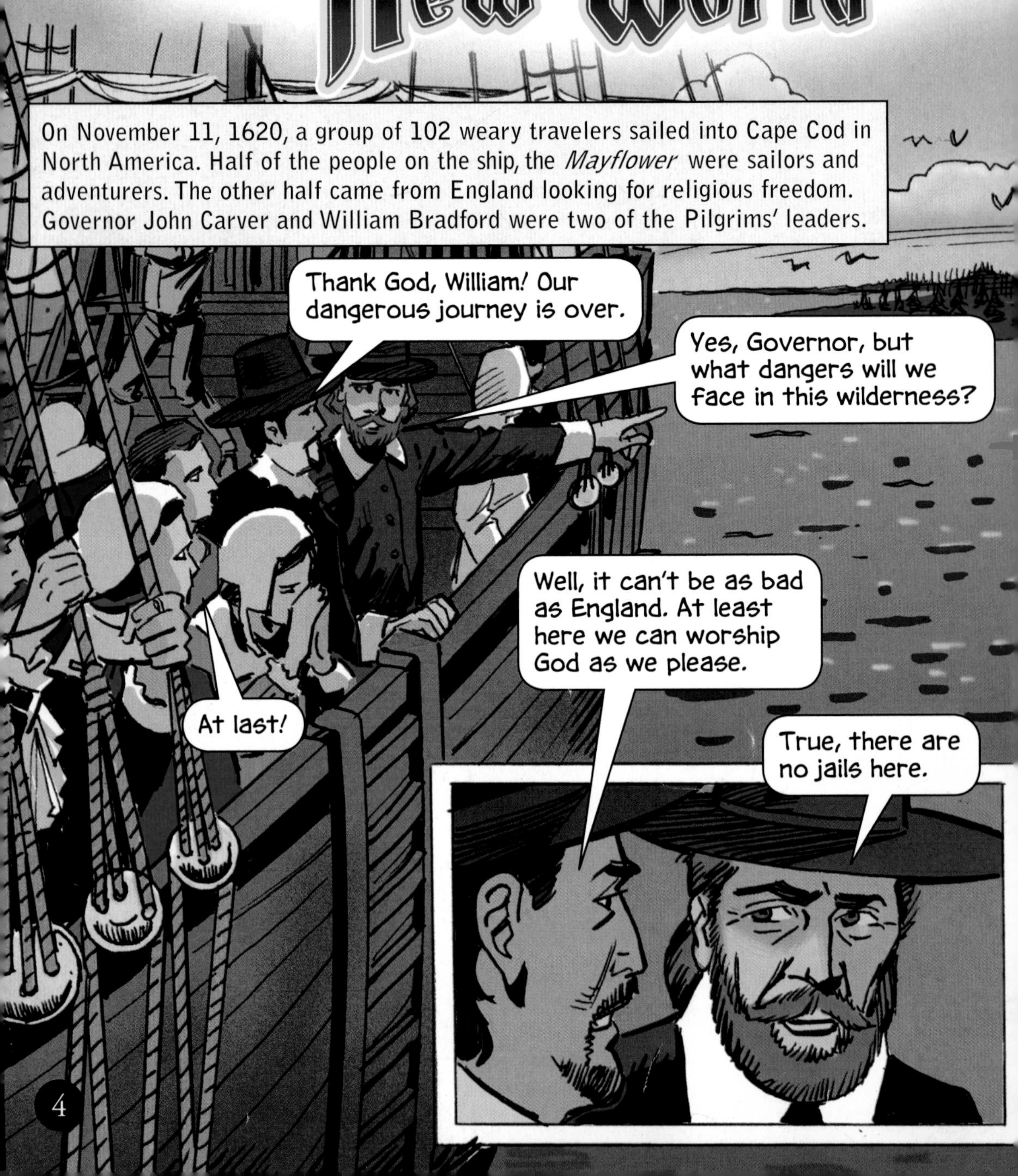
On November 11, 1620, a group of 102 weary travelers sailed into Cape Cod in North America. Half of the people on the ship, the *Mayflower* were sailors and adventurers. The other half came from England looking for religious freedom. Governor John Carver and William Bradford were two of the Pilgrims' leaders.
Thank God, William! Our dangerous journey is over.
Yes, Governor, but what dangers will we face in this wilderness?
At last!
Well, it can't be as bad as England. At least here we can worship God as we please.
True, there are no jails here.

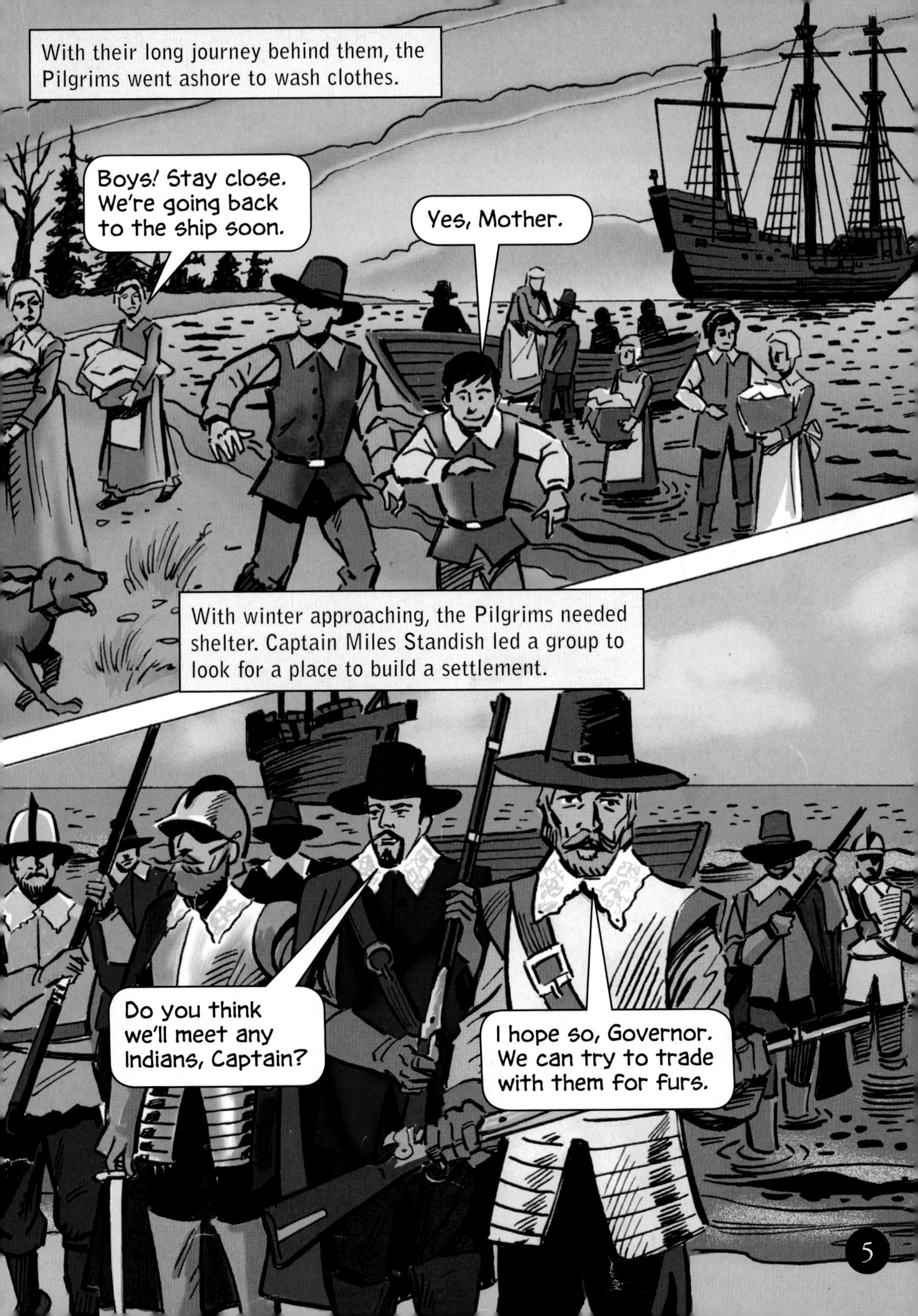
With their long journey behind them, the Pilgrims went ashore to wash clothes.
Boys! Stay close. We're going back to the ship soon.
Yes, Mother.
With winter approaching, the Pilgrims needed shelter. Captain Miles Standish led a group to look for a place to build a settlement.
Do you think we'll meet any Indians, Captain?
I hope so, Governor. We can try to trade with them for furs.

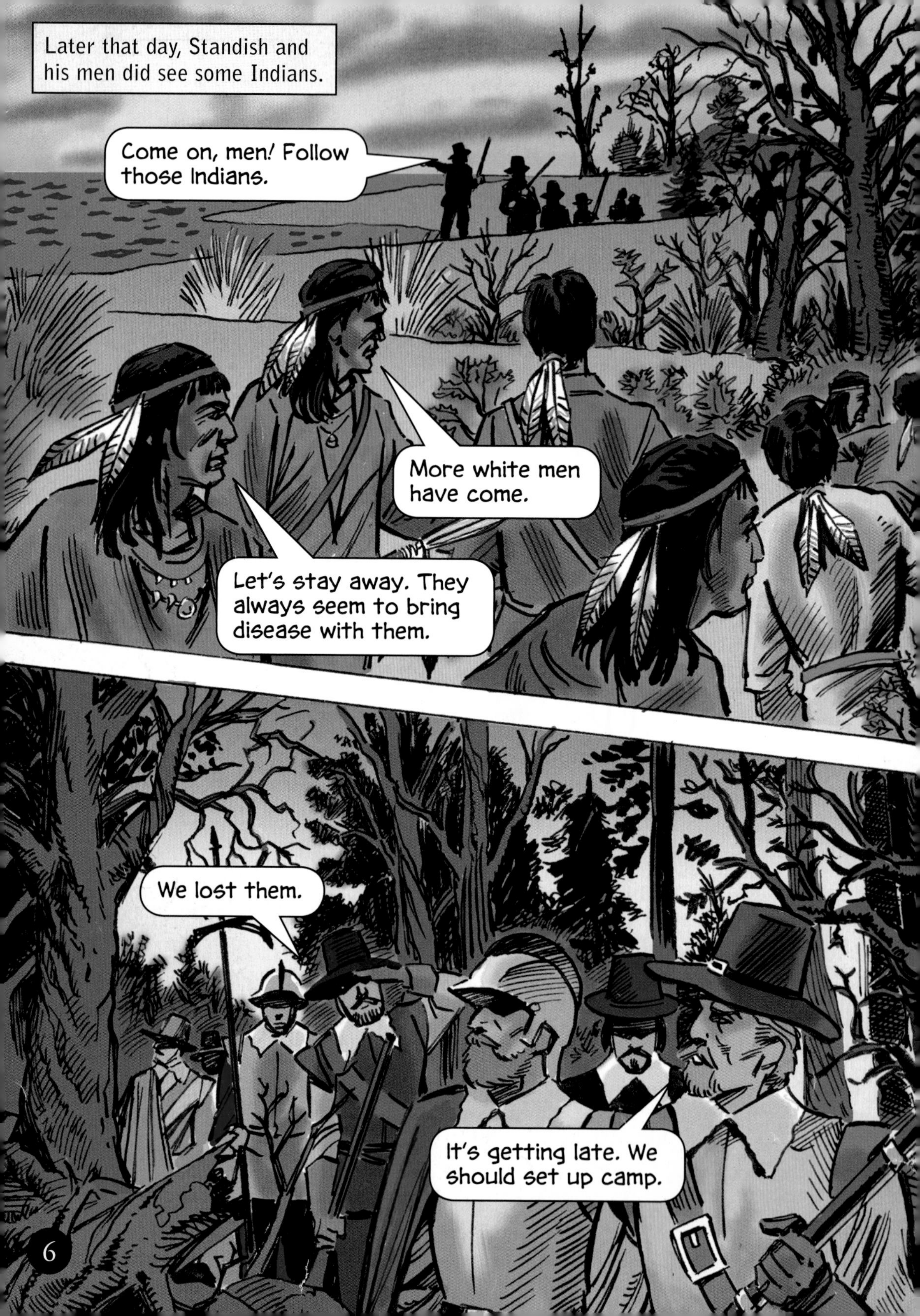
Later that day, Standish and his men did see some Indians.
Come on, men! Follow those Indians.
More white men have come.
Let's stay away. They always seem to bring disease with them.
We lost them.
It's getting late. We should set up camp.

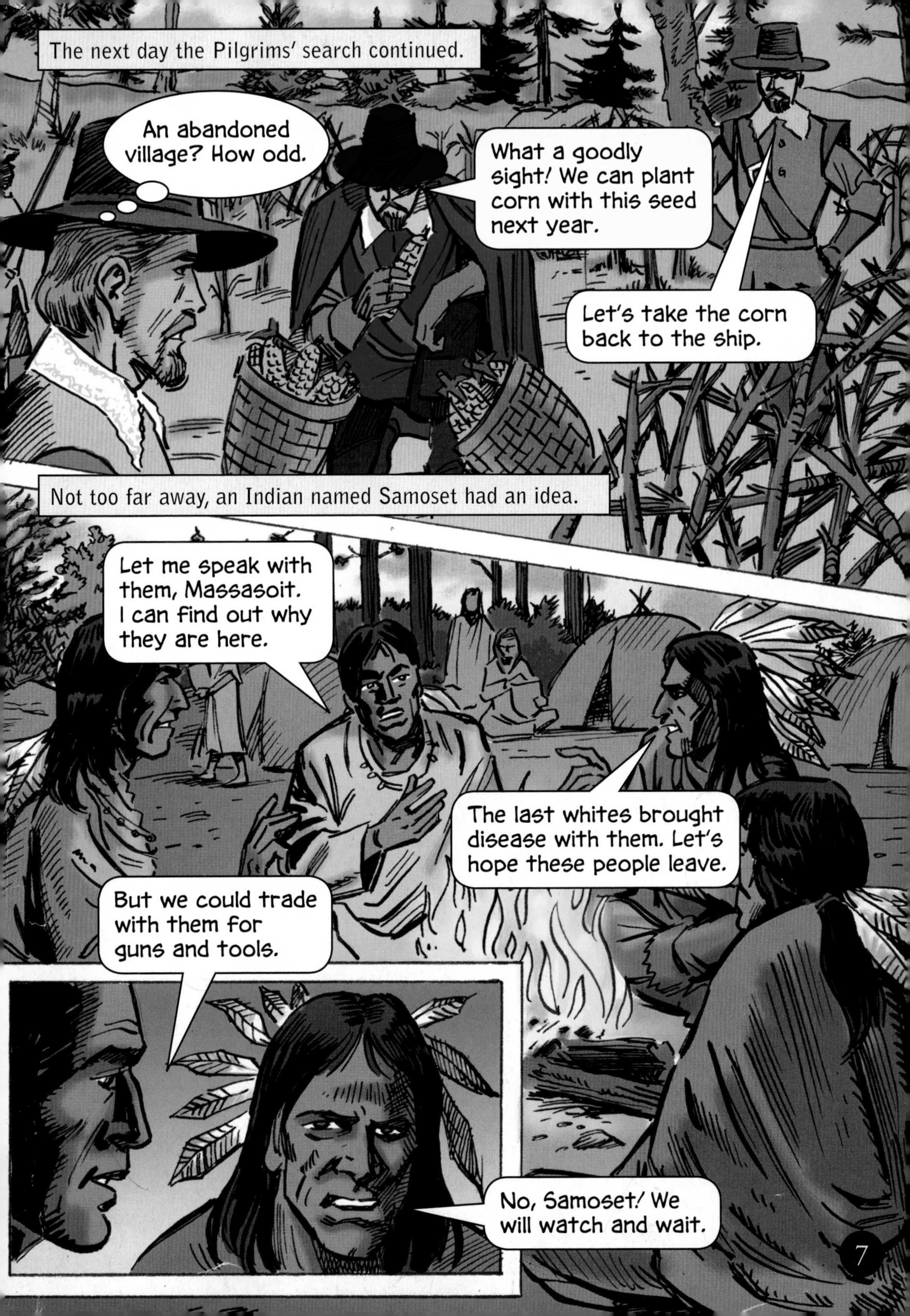
The next day the Pilgrims' search continued.
An abandoned village? How odd.
What a goodly sight! We can plant corn with this seed next year.
Let's take the corn back to the ship.
Not too far away, an Indian named Samoset had an idea.
Let me speak with them, Massasoit. I can find out why they are here.
The last whites brought disease with them. Let's hope these people leave.
But we could trade with them for guns and tools.
No, Samoset! We will watch and wait.

Chapter 2
The First Winter

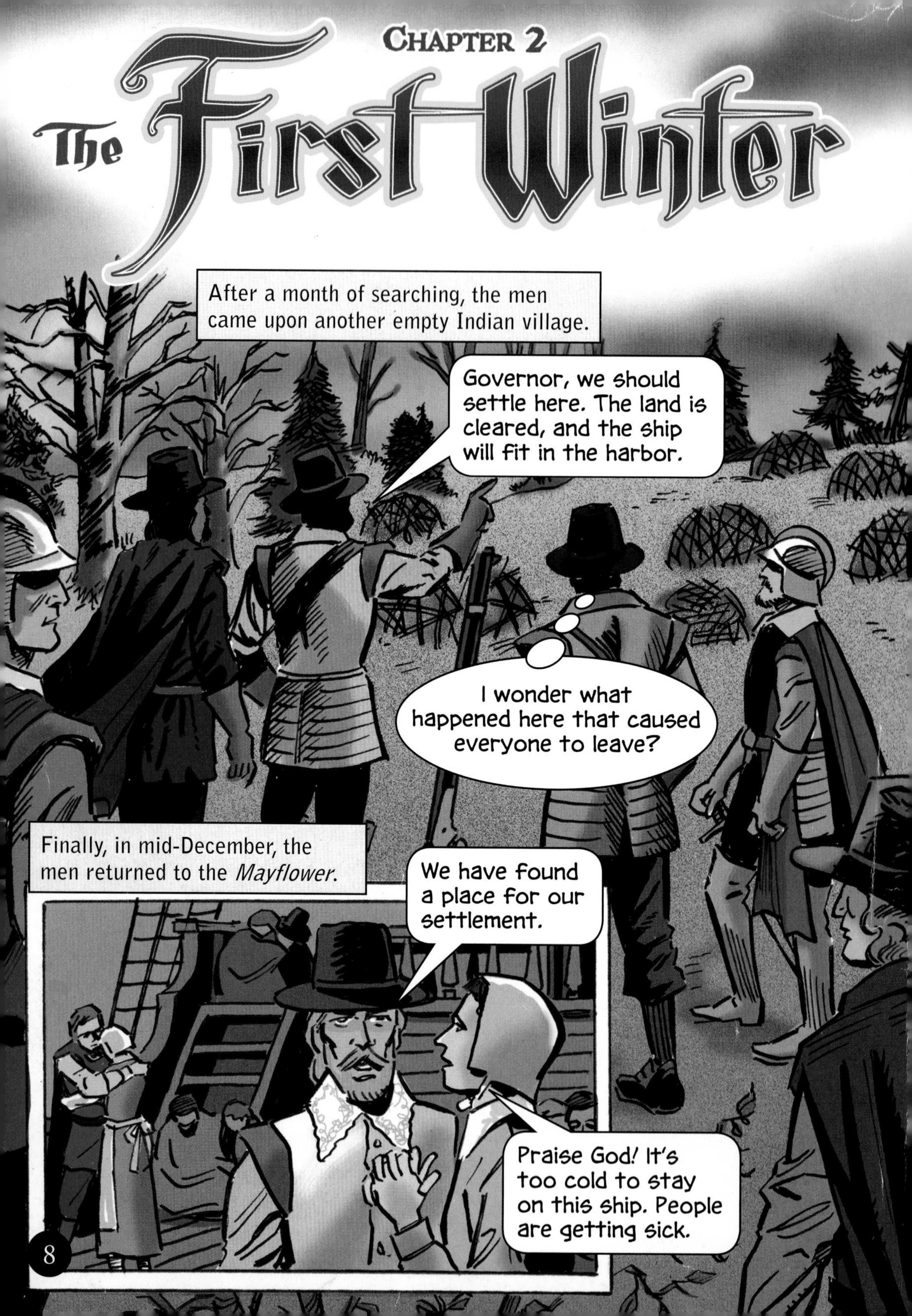
After a month of searching, the men came upon another empty Indian village.
Governor, we should settle here. The land is cleared, and the ship will fit in the harbor.
I wonder what happened here that caused everyone to leave?
Finally, in mid-December, the men returned to the *Mayflower*.
We have found a place for our settlement.
Praise God! It's too cold to stay on this ship. People are getting sick.

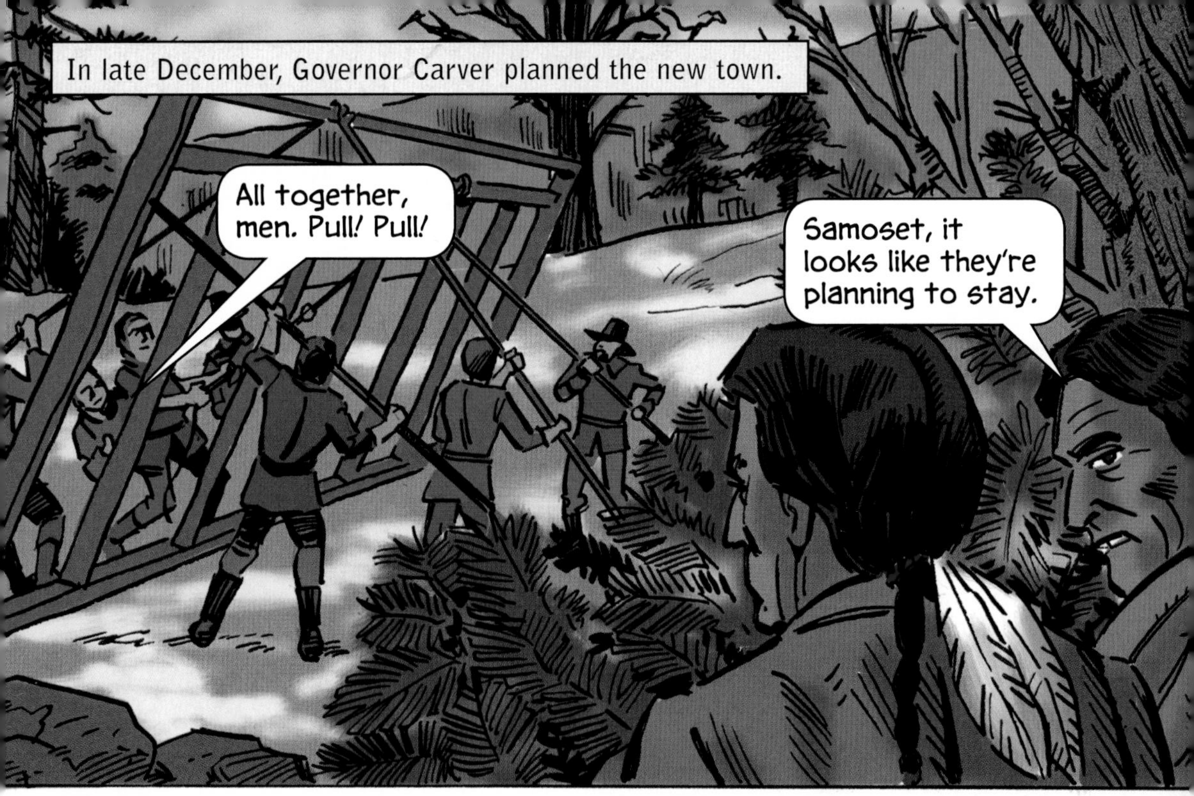
In late December, Governor Carver planned the new town.
All together, men. Pull! Pull!
Samoset, it looks like they're planning to stay.

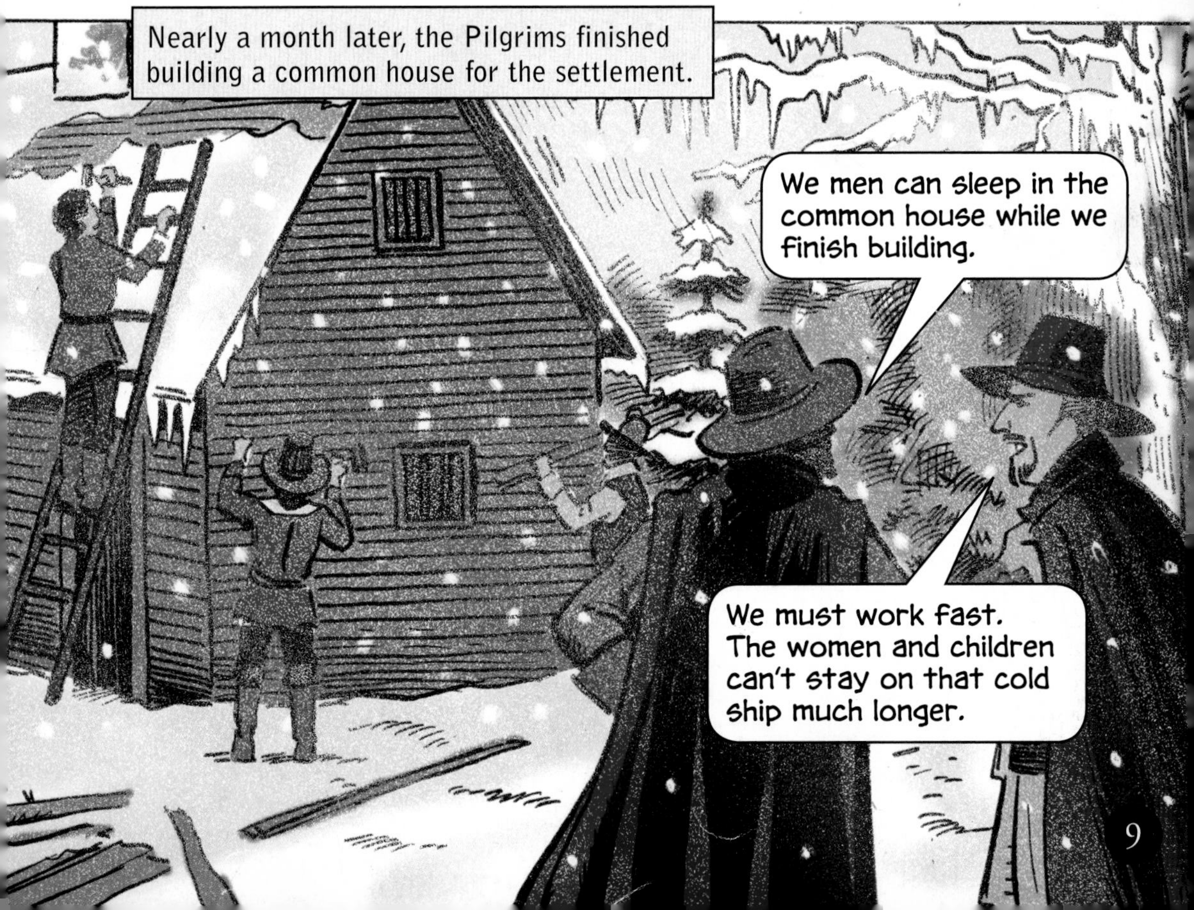
Nearly a month later, the Pilgrims finished building a common house for the settlement.
We men can sleep in the common house while we finish building.
We must work fast. The women and children can't stay on that cold ship much longer.

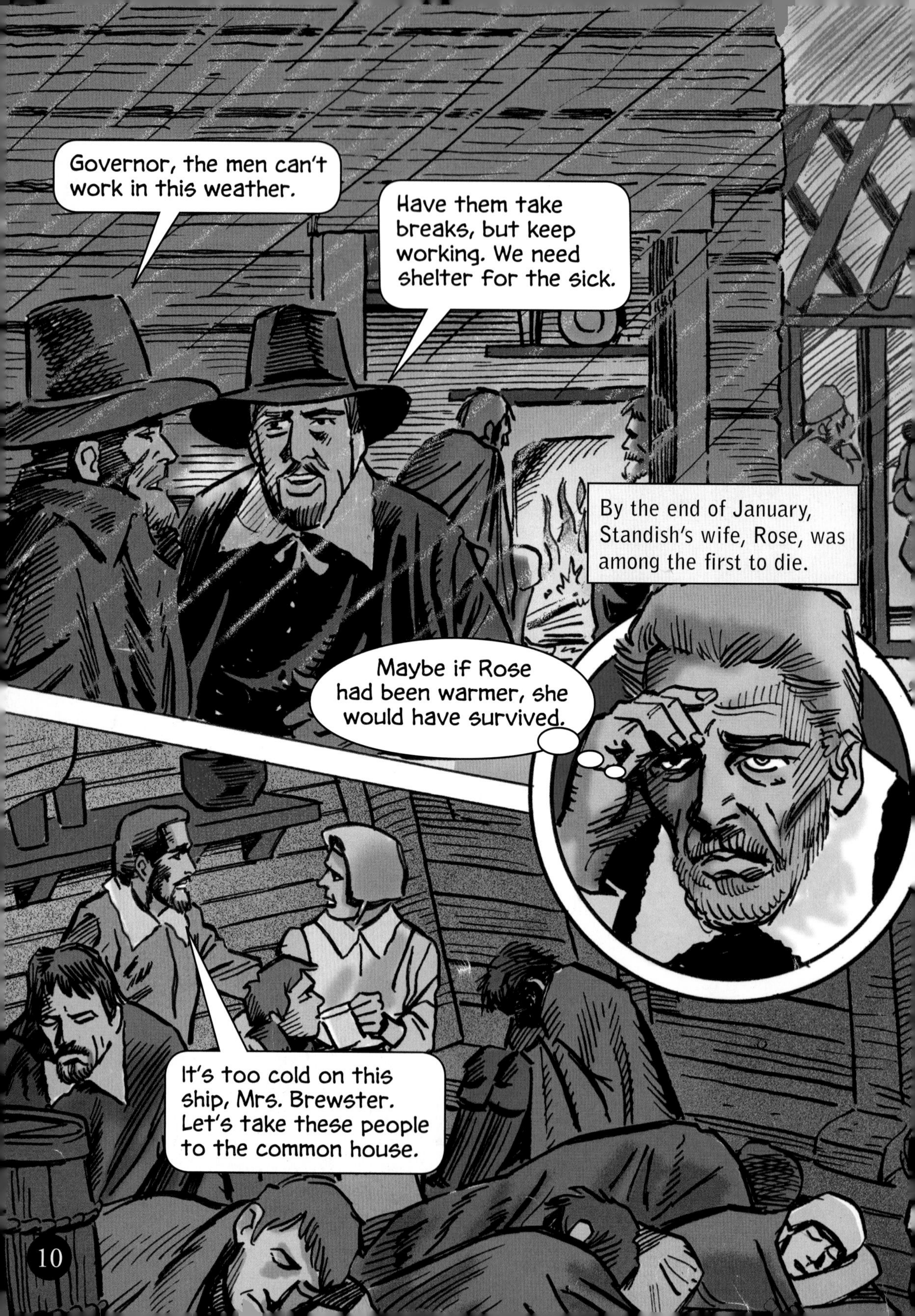
Governor, the men can't work in this weather.
Have them take breaks, but keep working. We need shelter for the sick.
By the end of January, Standish's wife, Rose, was among the first to die.
Maybe if Rose had been warmer, she would have survived.
It's too cold on this ship, Mrs. Brewster. Let's take these people to the common house.

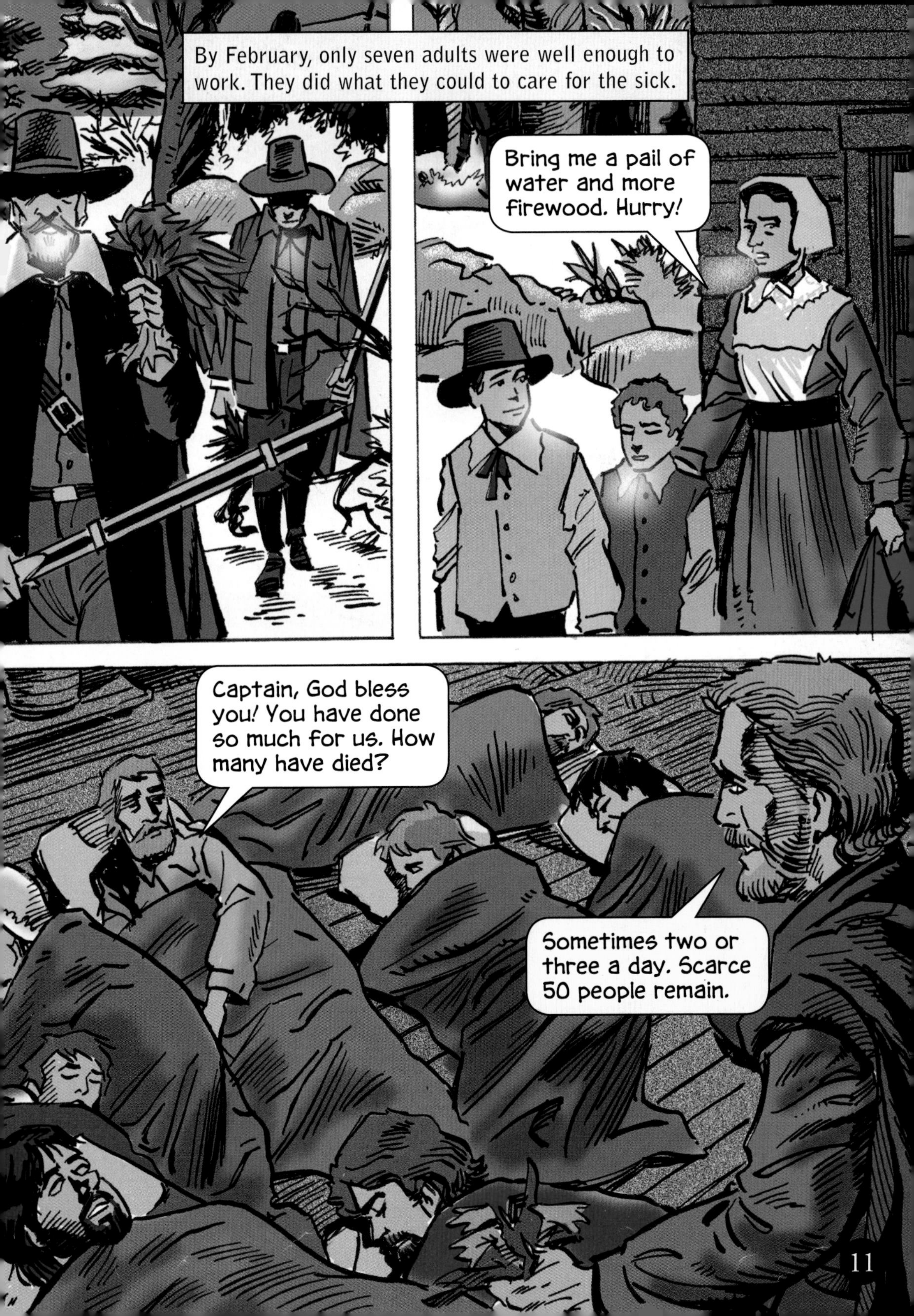
By February, only seven adults were well enough to work. They did what they could to care for the sick.
Bring me a pail of water and more firewood. Hurry!
Captain, God bless you! You have done so much for us. How many have died?
Sometimes two or three a day. Scarce 50 people remain.

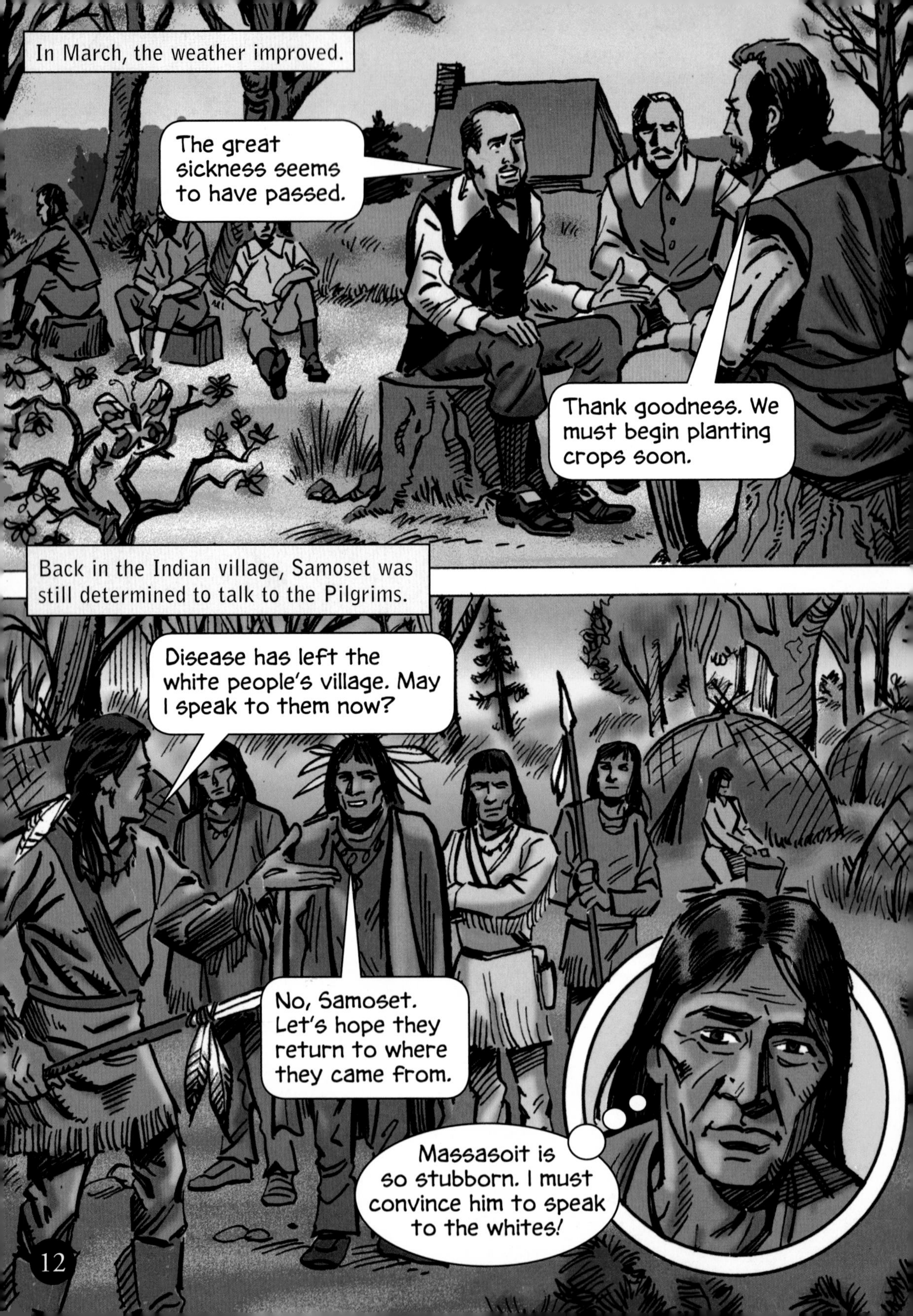
In March, the weather improved.
The great sickness seems to have passed.
Thank goodness. We must begin planting crops soon.
Back in the Indian village, Samoset was still determined to talk to the Pilgrims.
Disease has left the white people's village. May I speak to them now?
No, Samoset. Let's hope they return to where they came from.
Massasoit is so stubborn. I must convince him to speak to the whites!

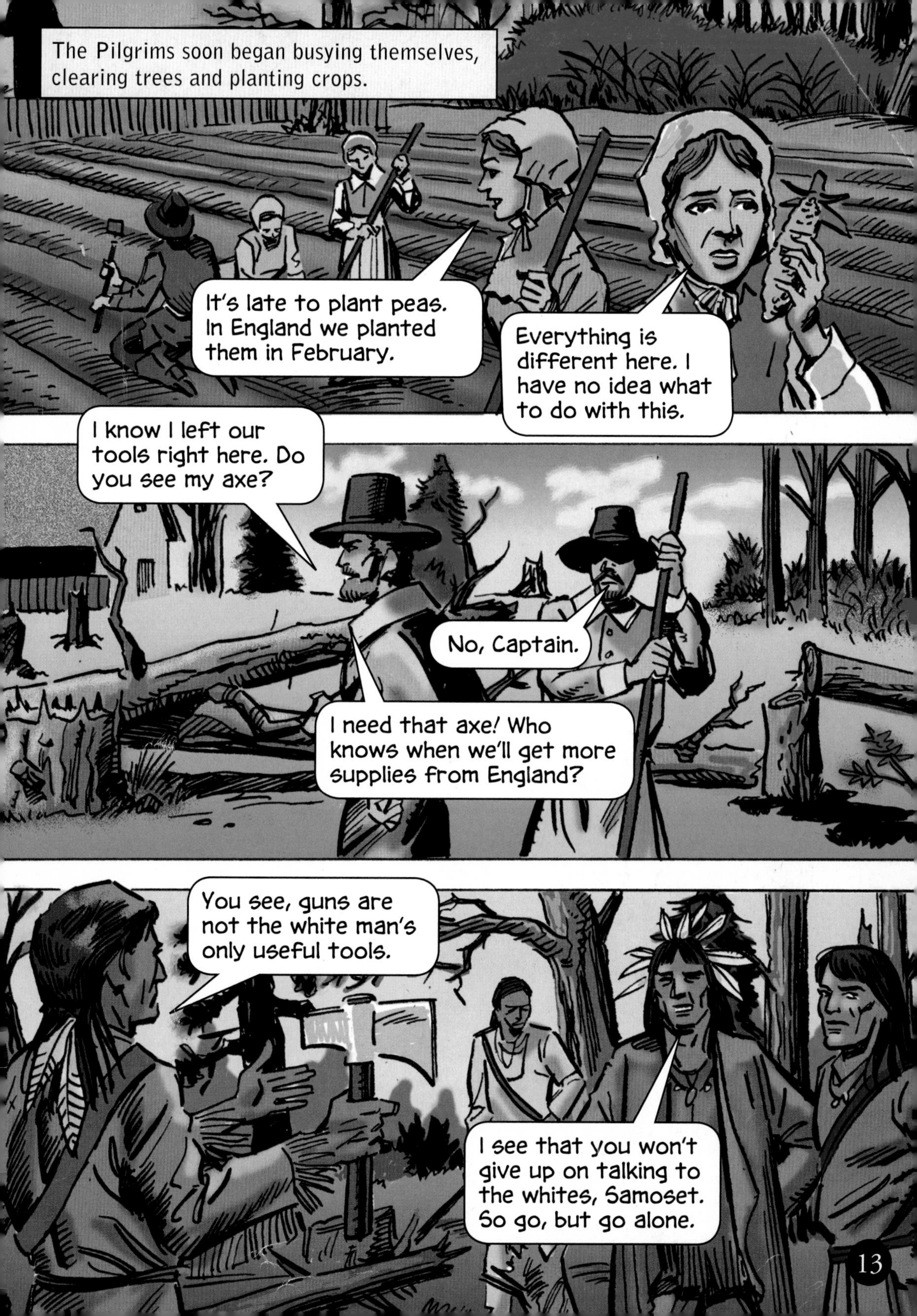
The Pilgrims soon began busying themselves, clearing trees and planting crops.
It's late to plant peas. In England we planted them in February.
Everything is different here. I have no idea what to do with this.
I know I left our tools right here. Do you see my axe?
No, Captain.
I need that axe! Who knows when we'll get more supplies from England?
You see, guns are not the white man's only useful tools.
I see that you won't give up on talking to the whites, Samoset. So go, but go alone.

Chapter 3

Meeting the Indians

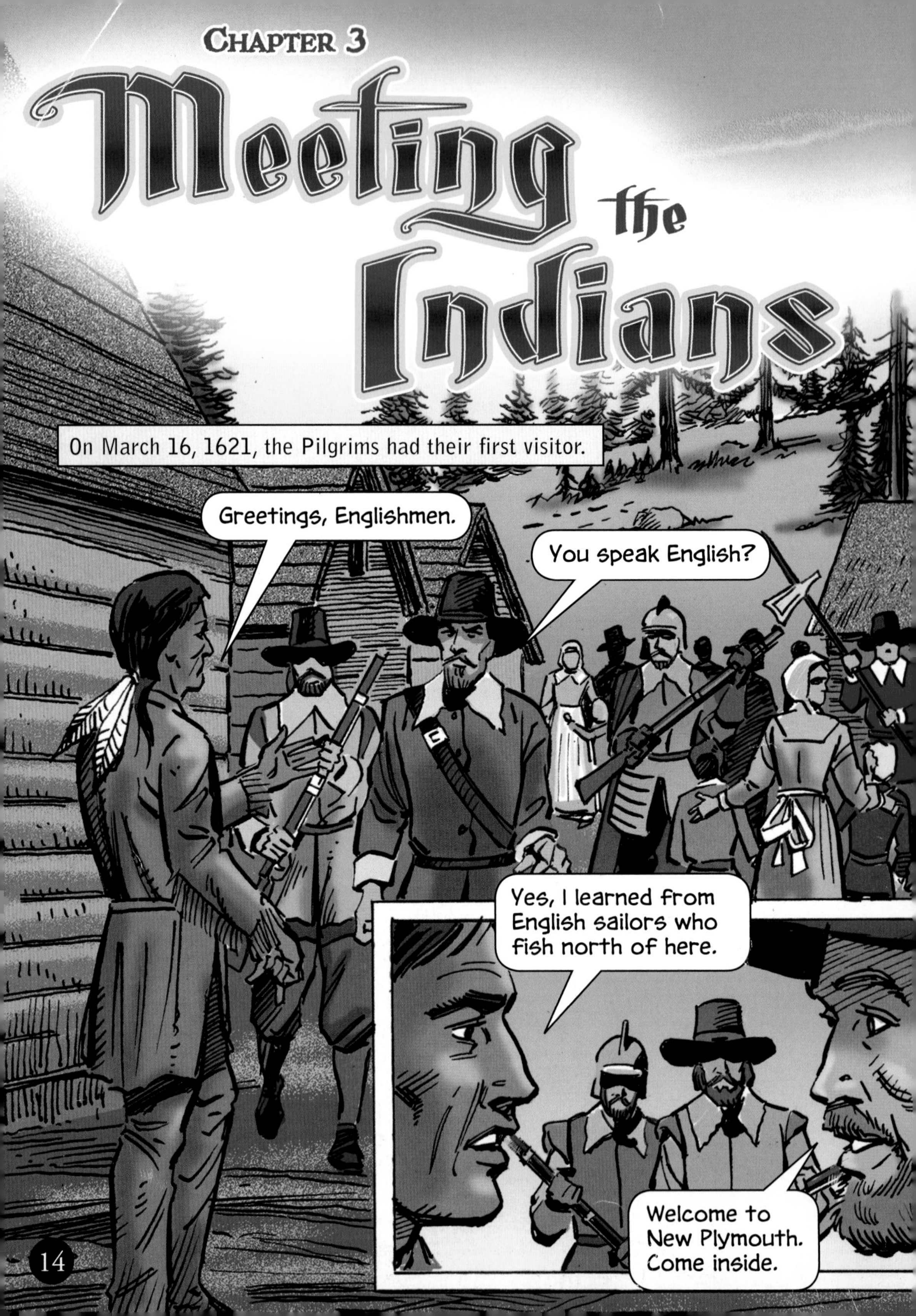
On March 16, 1621, the Pilgrims had their first visitor.
Greetings, Englishmen.
You speak English?
Yes, I learned from English sailors who fish north of here.
Welcome to New Plymouth. Come inside.

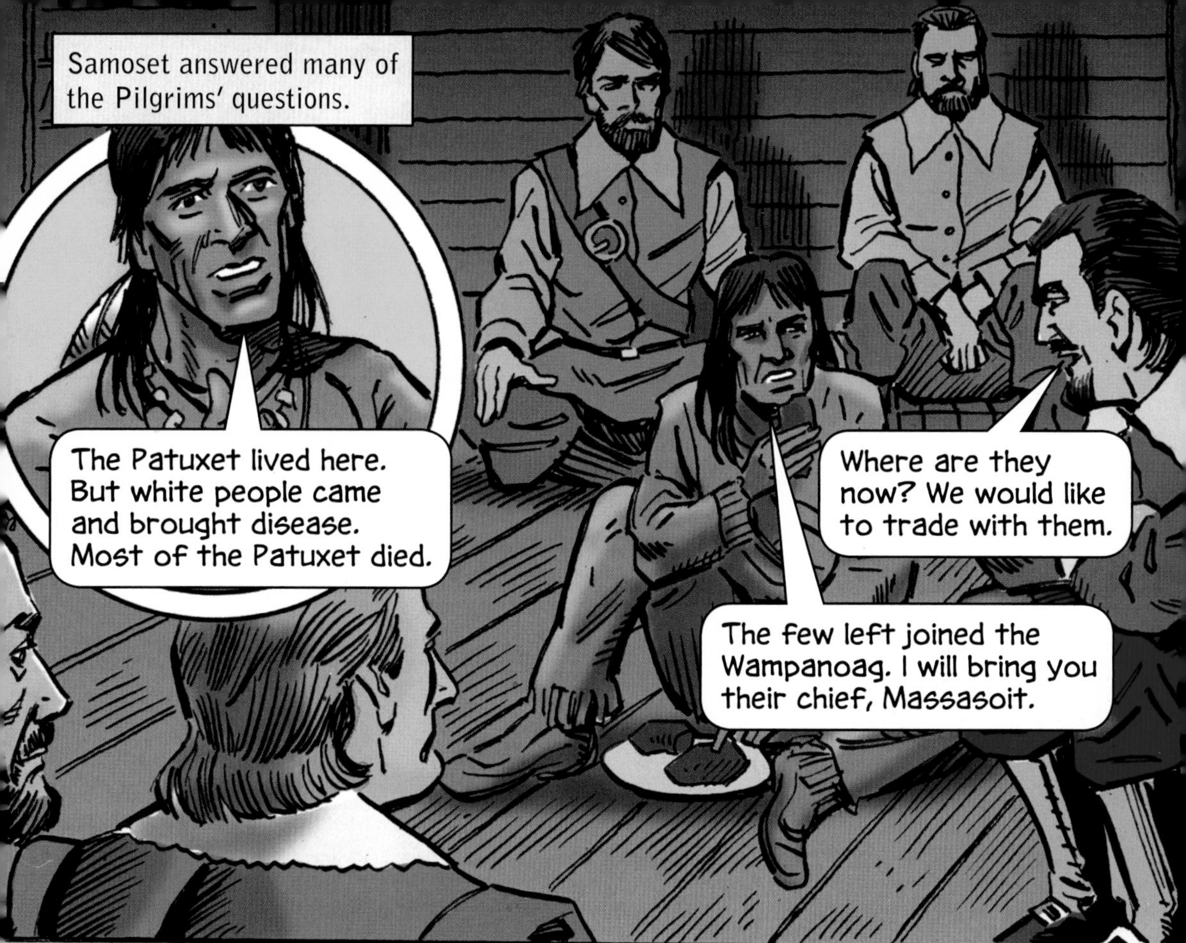
Samoset answered many of the Pilgrims' questions.
The Patuxet lived here. But white people came and brought disease. Most of the Patuxet died.
Where are they now? We would like to trade with them.
The few left joined the Wampanoag. I will bring you their chief, Massasoit.

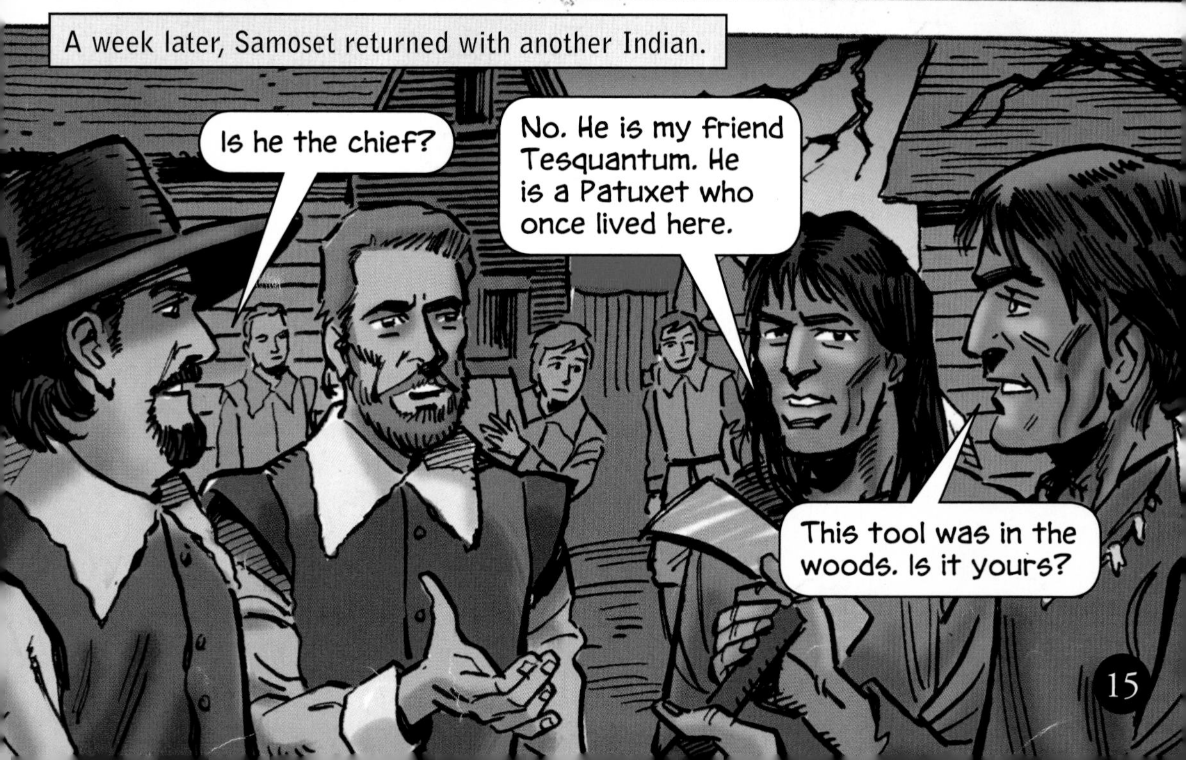
A week later, Samoset returned with another Indian.
Is he the chief?
No. He is my friend Tesquantum. He is a Patuxet who once lived here.
This tool was in the woods. Is it yours?

How is it that you speak English, Tes-quan-ummm . . . Squanto?

I have spent much time with Englishmen.

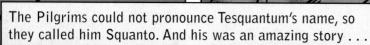

The Pilgrims could not pronounce Tesquantum's name, so they called him Squanto. And his was an amazing story . . .

. . . of capture . . .

. . . and slavery . . .

. . . and all the while, trying to get back home.

And when I came back, my people were gone.

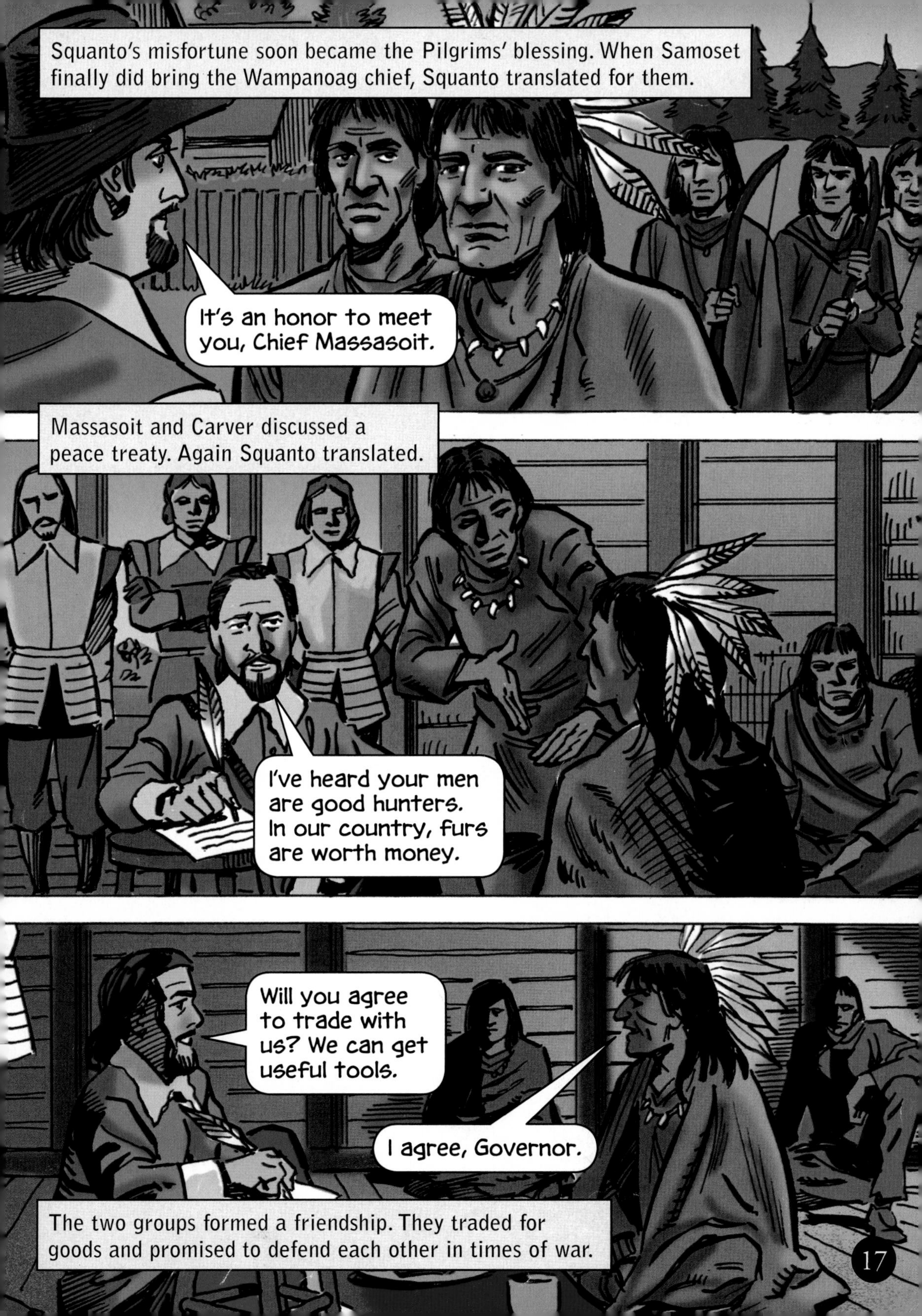
Squanto's misfortune soon became the Pilgrims' blessing. When Samoset finally did bring the Wampanoag chief, Squanto translated for them.
It's an honor to meet you, Chief Massasoit.
Massasoit and Carver discussed a peace treaty. Again Squanto translated.
I've heard your men are good hunters. In our country, furs are worth money.
Will you agree to trade with us? We can get useful tools.
I agree, Governor.
The two groups formed a friendship. They traded for goods and promised to defend each other in times of war.

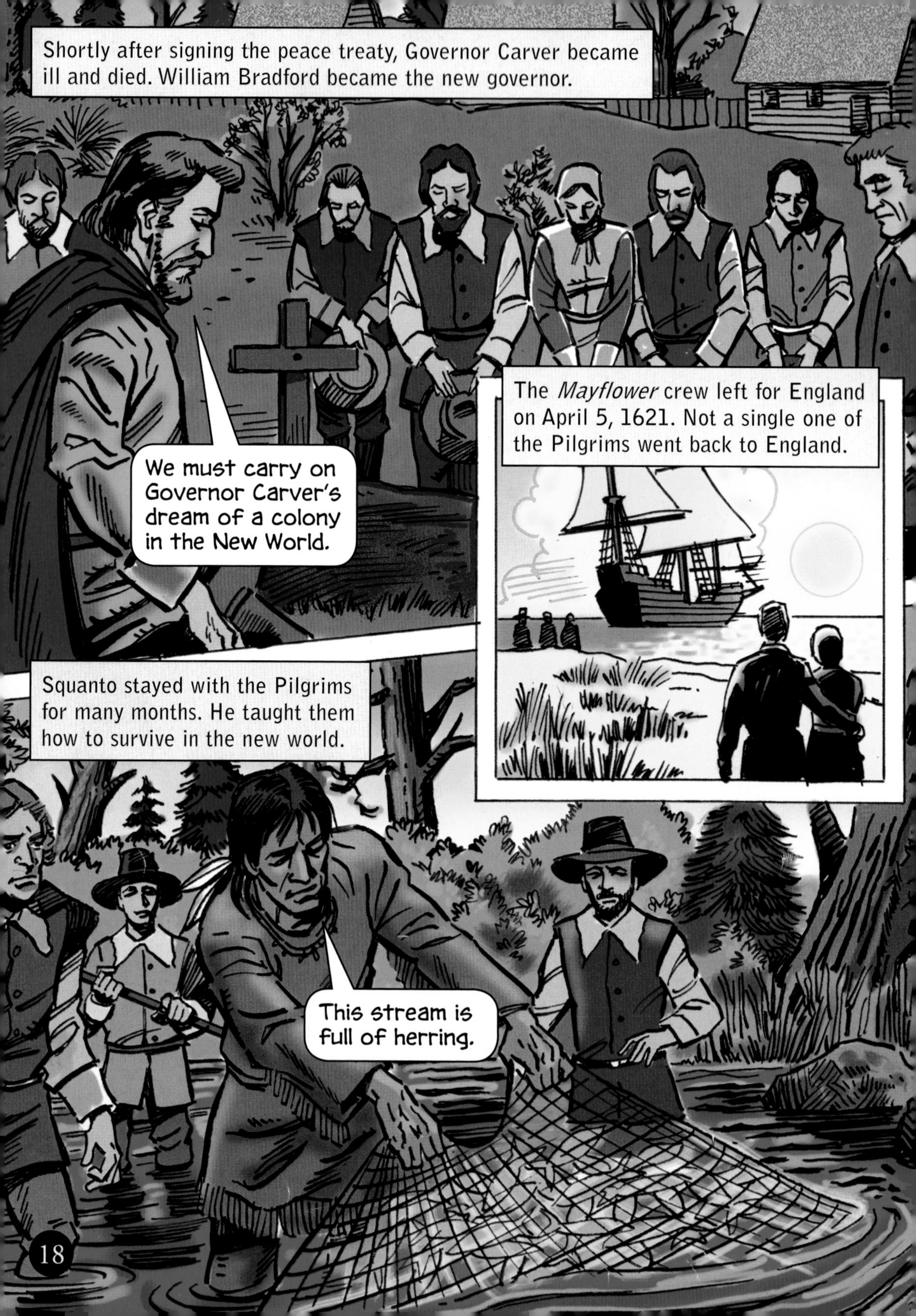

Shortly after signing the peace treaty, Governor Carver became ill and died. William Bradford became the new governor.
We must carry on Governor Carver's dream of a colony in the New World.
The *Mayflower* crew left for England on April 5, 1621. Not a single one of the Pilgrims went back to England.
Squanto stayed with the Pilgrims for many months. He taught them how to survive in the new world.
This stream is full of herring.

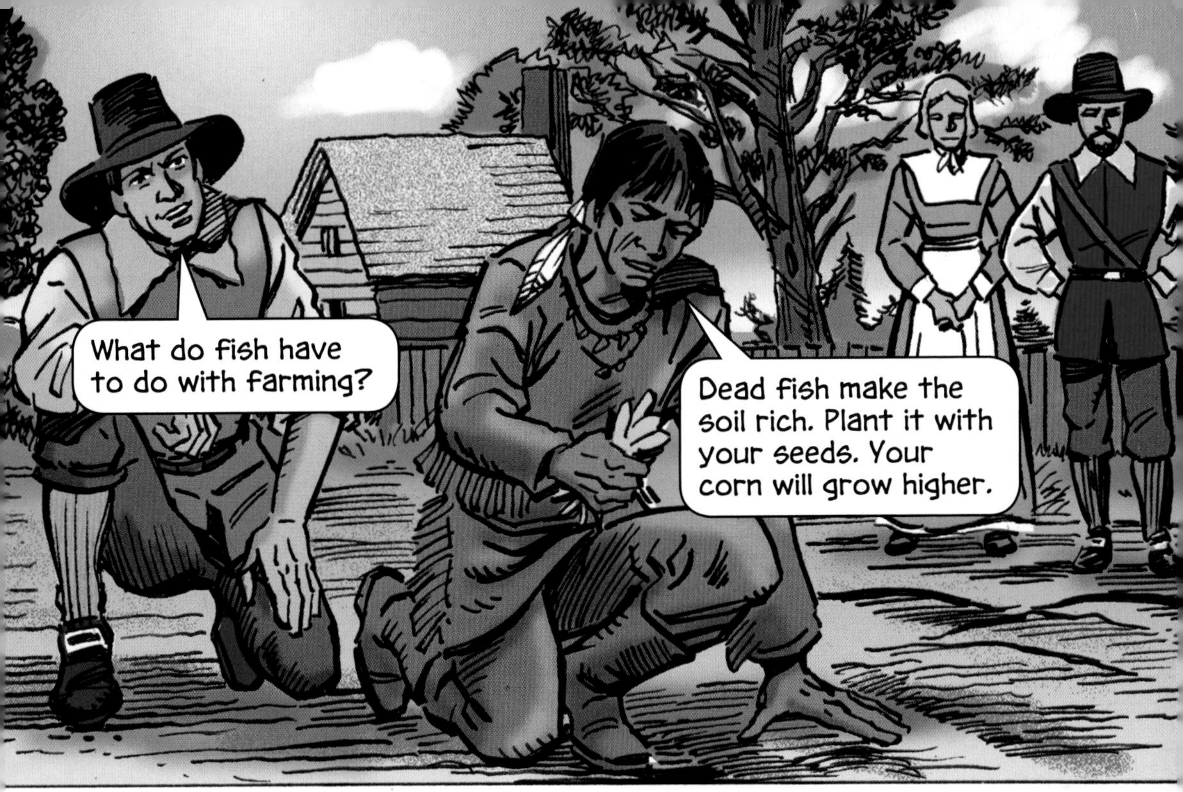
What do fish have to do with farming?
Dead fish make the soil rich. Plant it with your seeds. Your corn will grow higher.

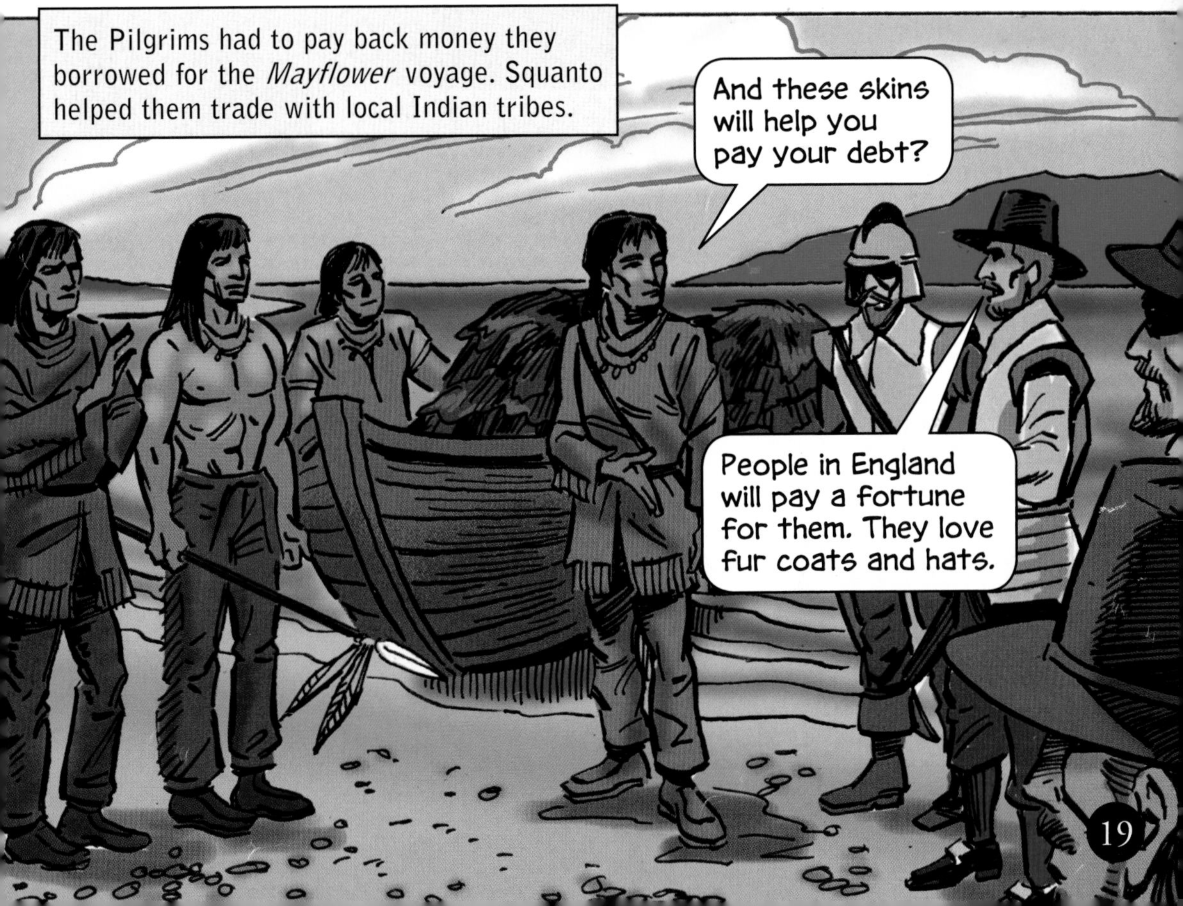
The Pilgrims had to pay back money they borrowed for the *Mayflower* voyage. Squanto helped them trade with local Indian tribes.
And these skins will help you pay your debt?
People in England will pay a fortune for them. They love fur coats and hats.

Chapter 4

The Harvest Feast

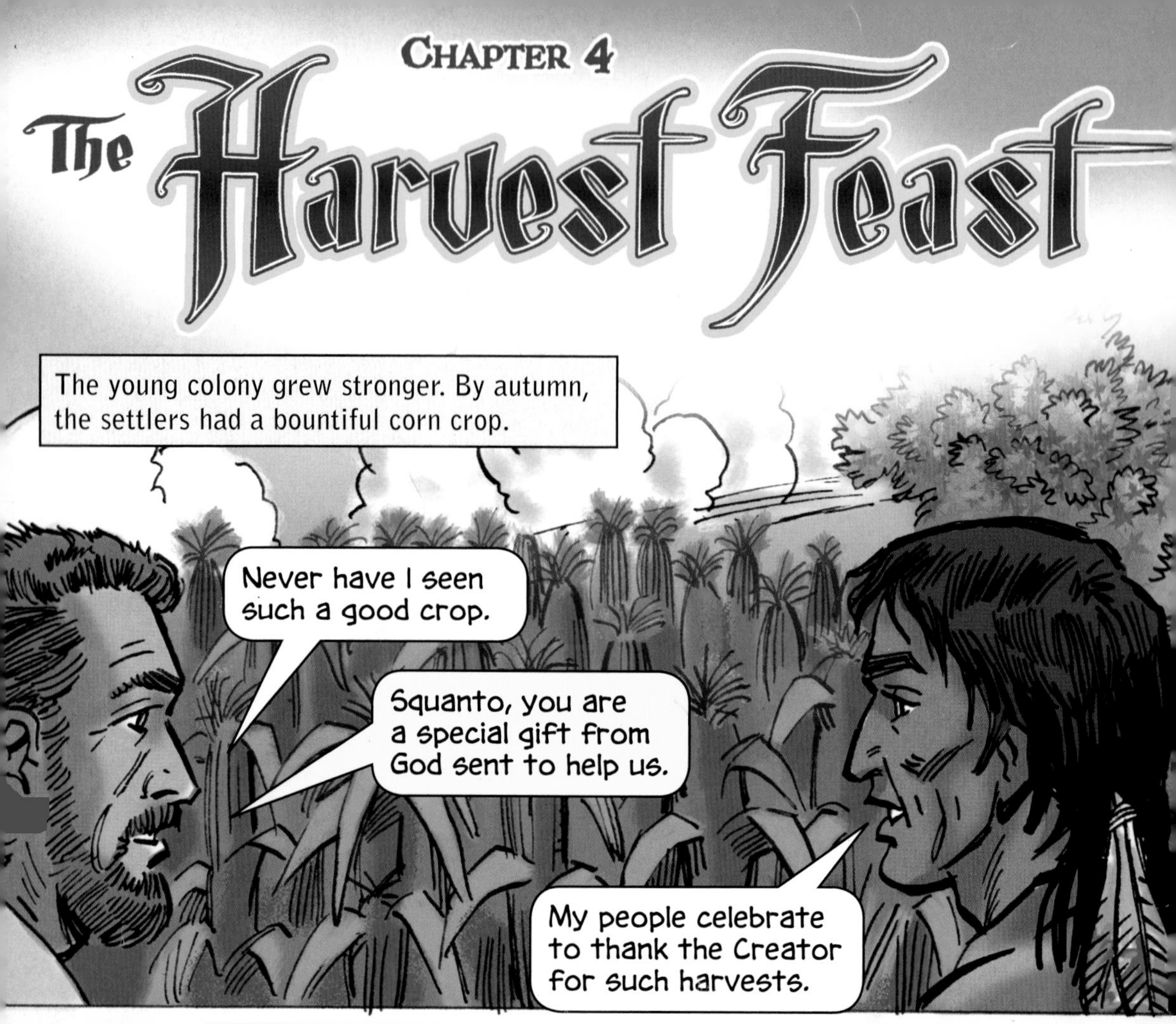
The young colony grew stronger. By autumn, the settlers had a bountiful corn crop.
Never have I seen such a good crop.
Squanto, you are a special gift from God sent to help us.
My people celebrate to thank the Creator for such harvests.

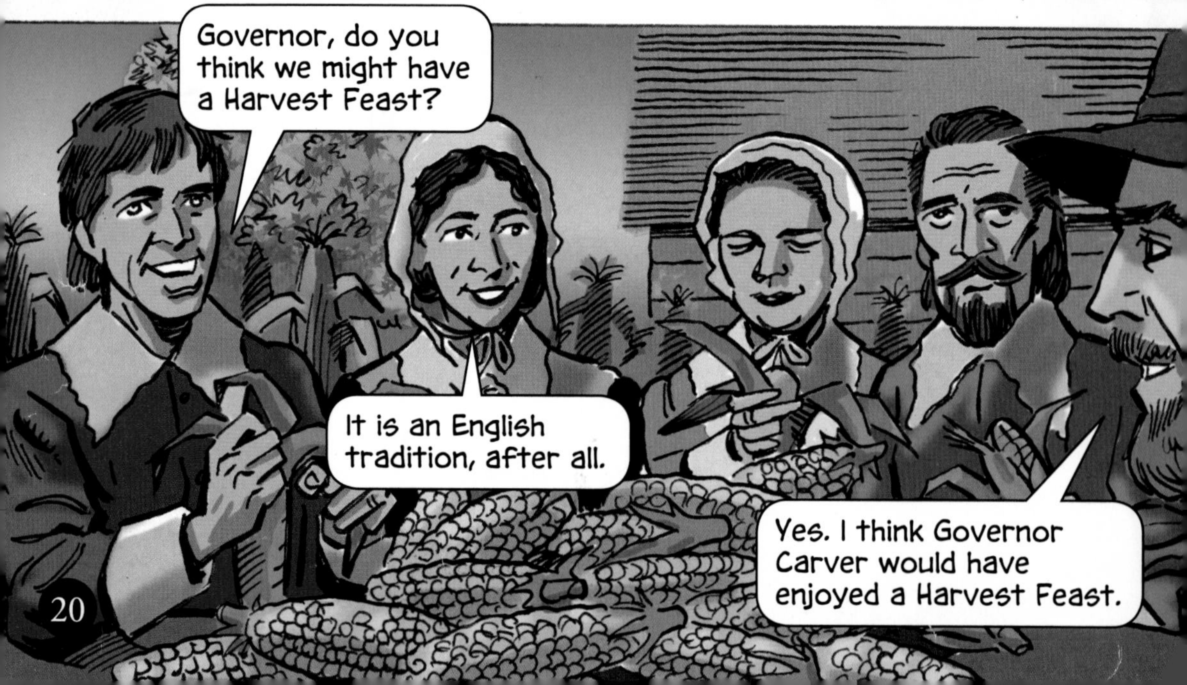
Governor, do you think we might have a Harvest Feast?
It is an English tradition, after all.
Yes. I think Governor Carver would have enjoyed a Harvest Feast.

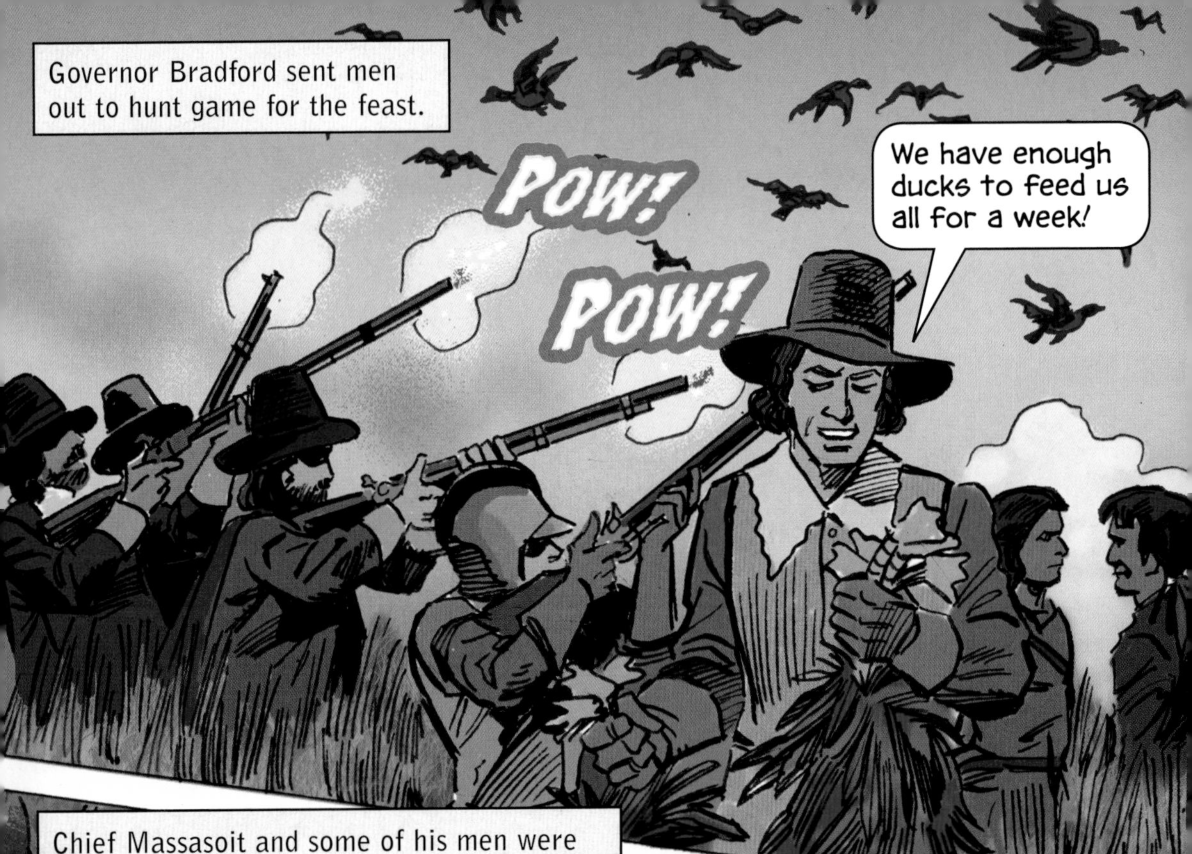
Governor Bradford sent men out to hunt game for the feast.
POW!
POW!
We have enough ducks to feed us all for a week!

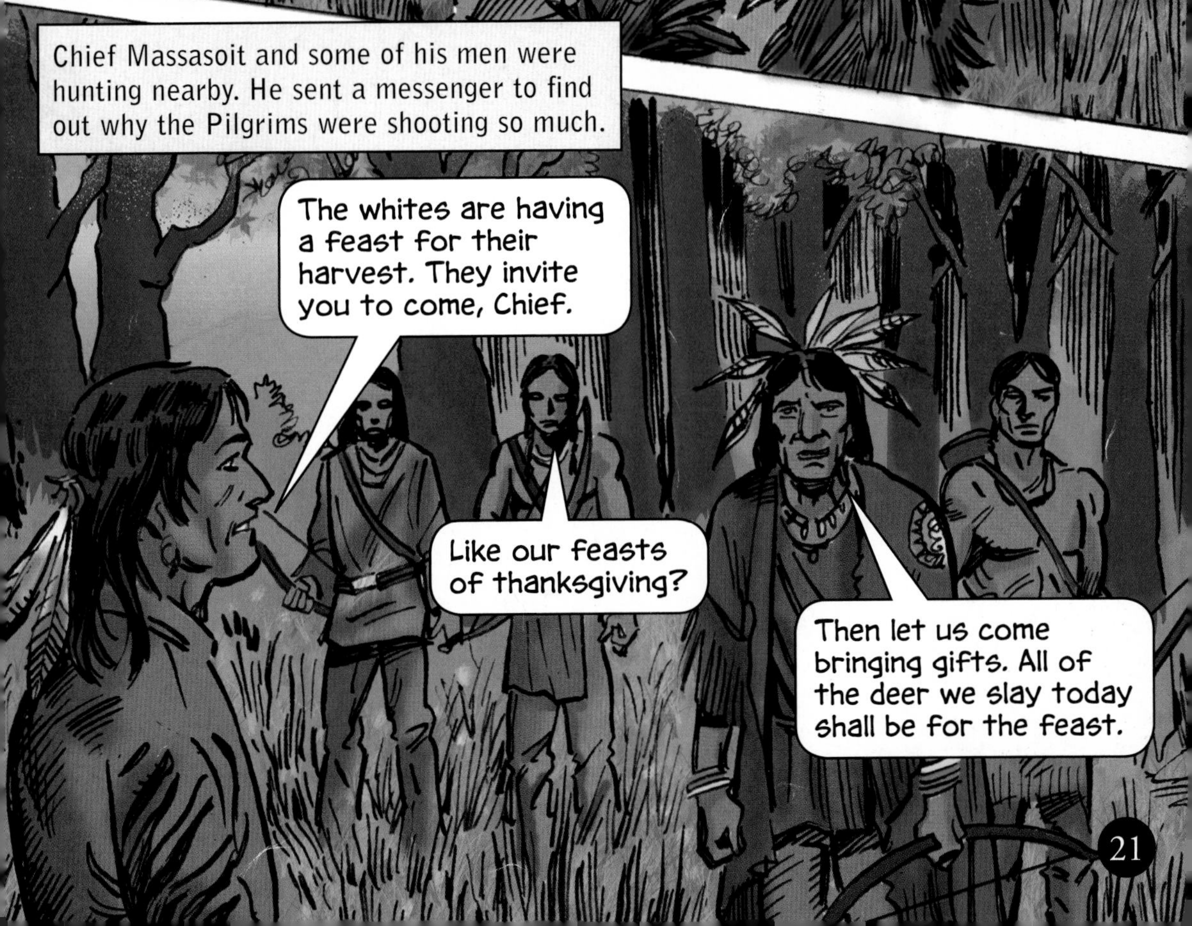
Chief Massasoit and some of his men were hunting nearby. He sent a messenger to find out why the Pilgrims were shooting so much.
The whites are having a feast for their harvest. They invite you to come, Chief.
Like our feasts of thanksgiving?
Then let us come bringing gifts. All of the deer we slay today shall be for the feast.

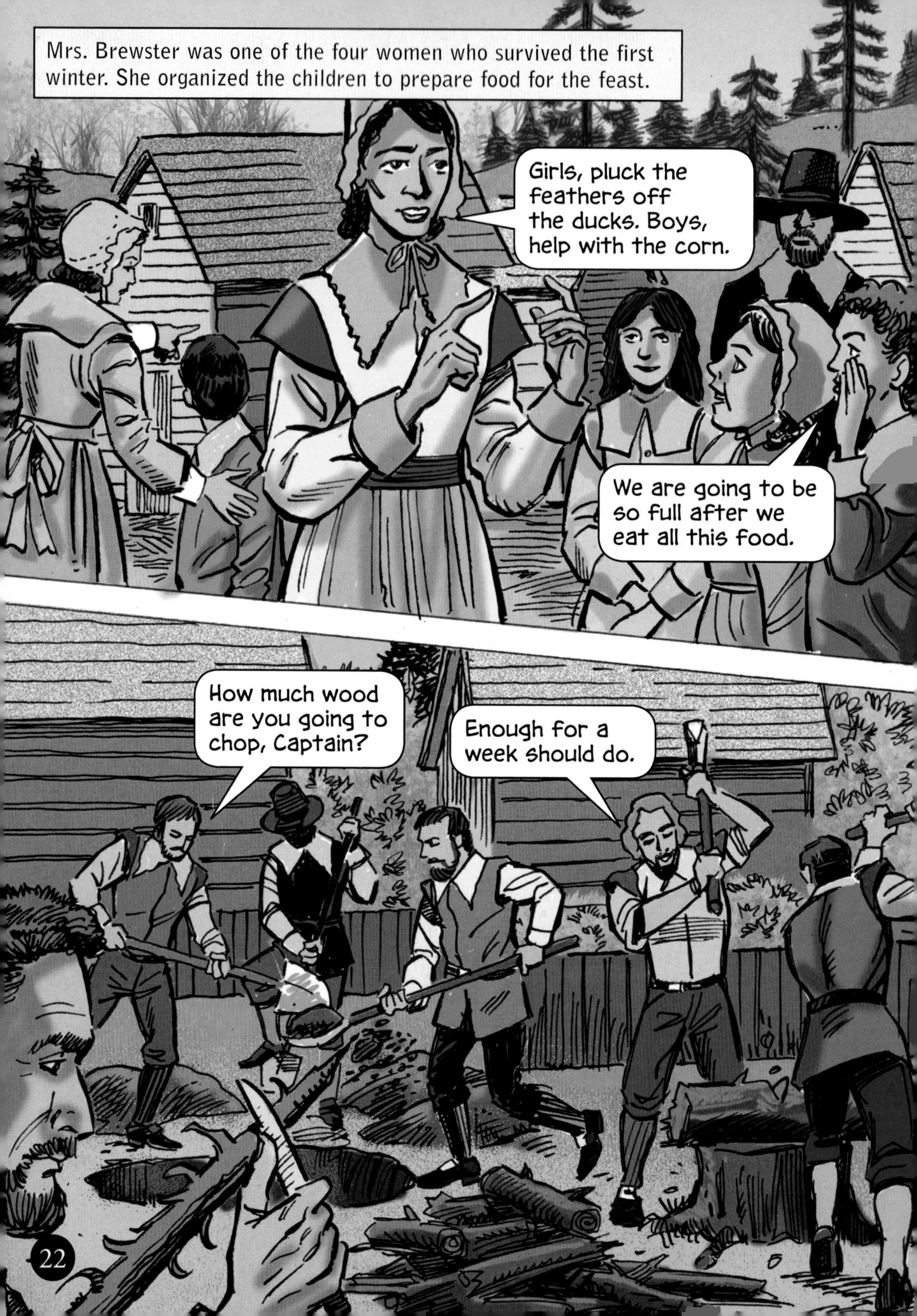
Mrs. Brewster was one of the four women who survived the first winter. She organized the children to prepare food for the feast.
Girls, pluck the feathers off the ducks. Boys, help with the corn.
We are going to be so full after we eat all this food.
How much wood are you going to chop, Captain?
Enough for a week should do.

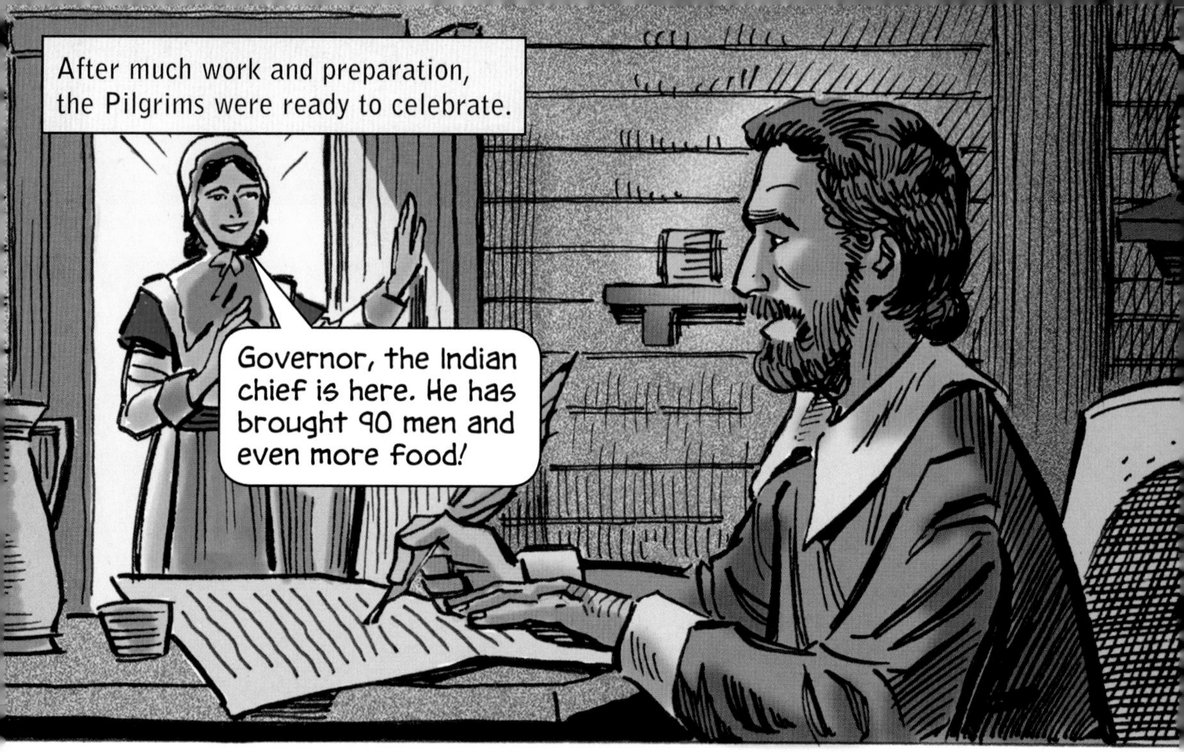
After much work and preparation, the Pilgrims were ready to celebrate.
Governor, the Indian chief is here. He has brought 90 men and even more food!

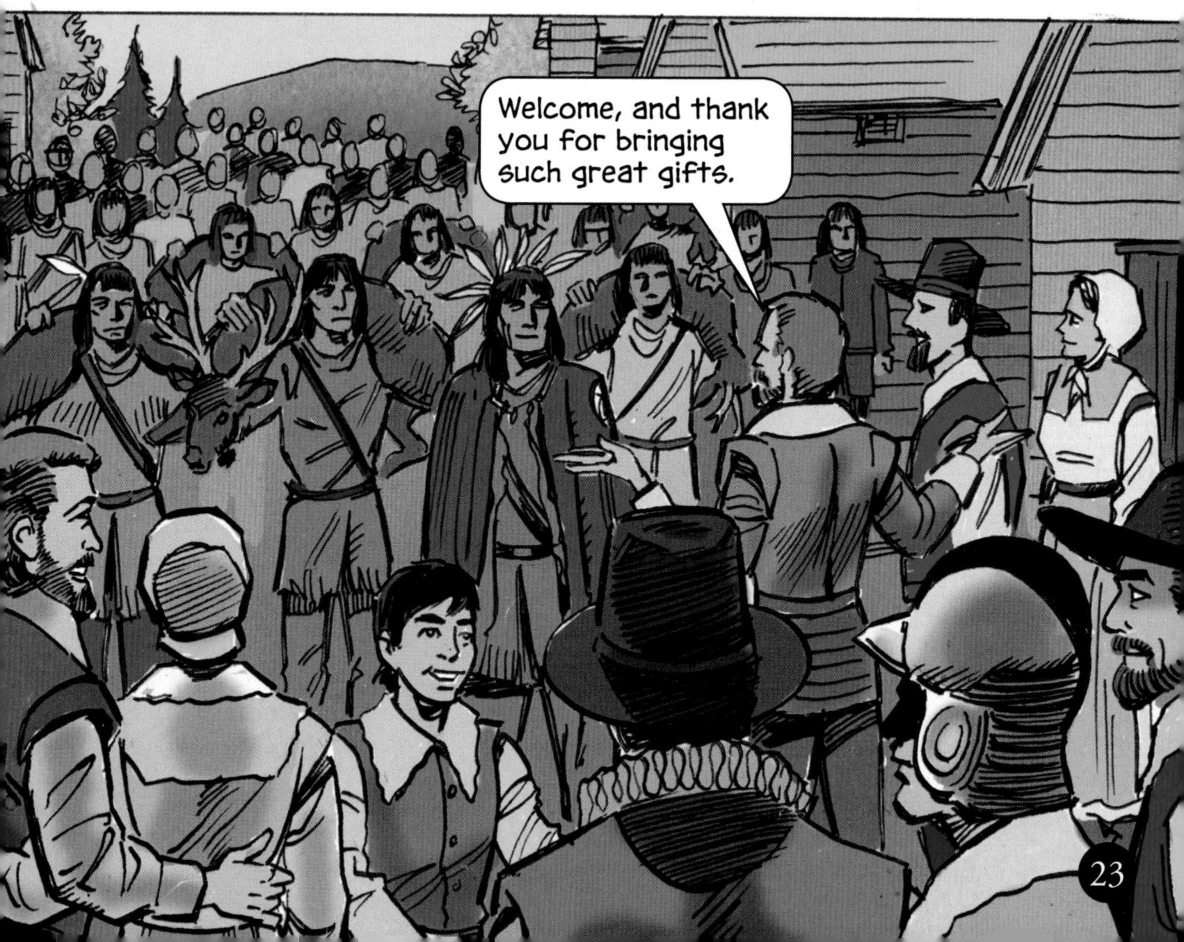
Welcome, and thank you for bringing such great gifts.

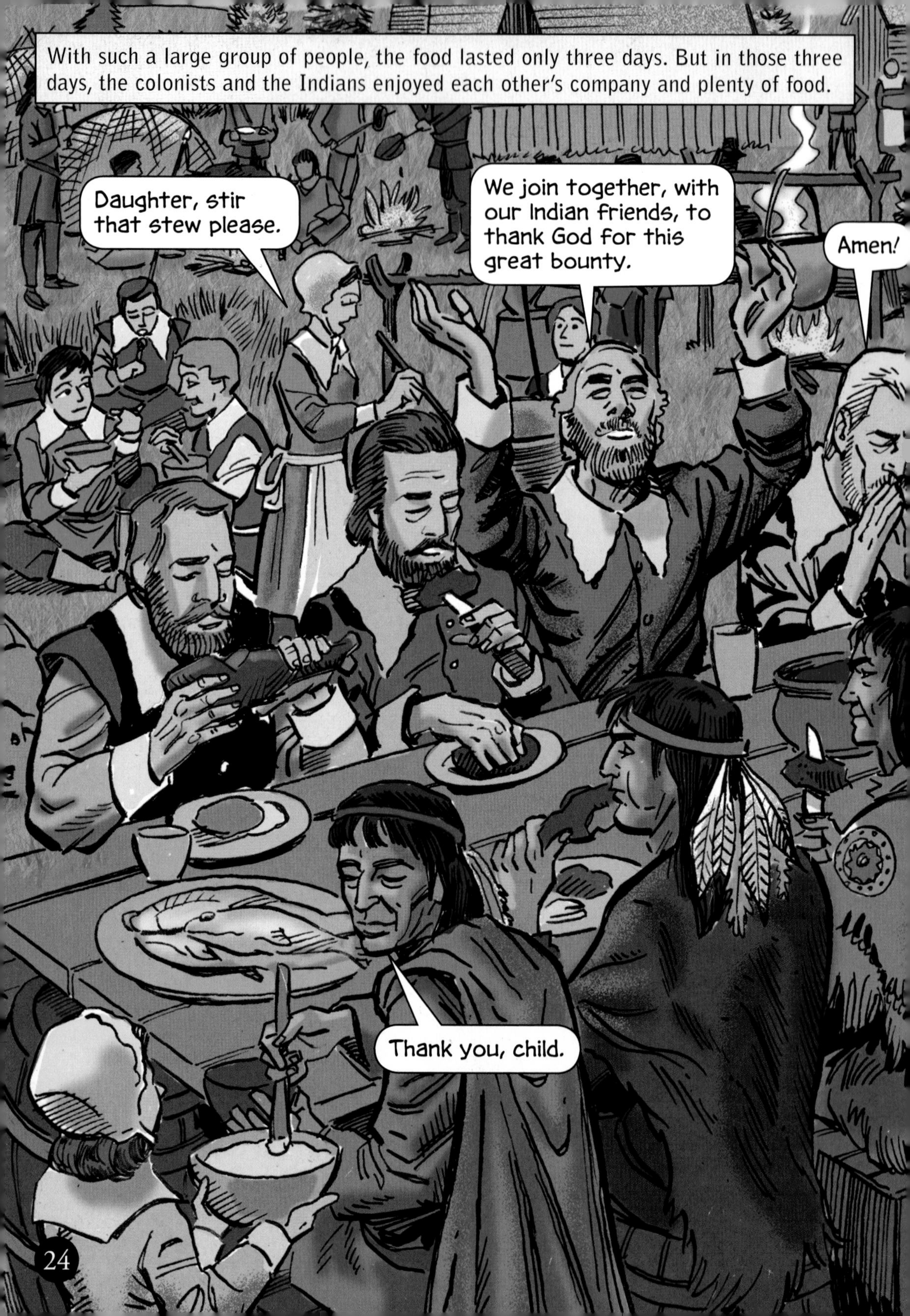
With such a large group of people, the food lasted only three days. But in those three days, the colonists and the Indians enjoyed each other's company and plenty of food.
Daughter, stir that stew please.
We join together, with our Indian friends, to thank God for this great bounty.
Amen!
Thank you, child.

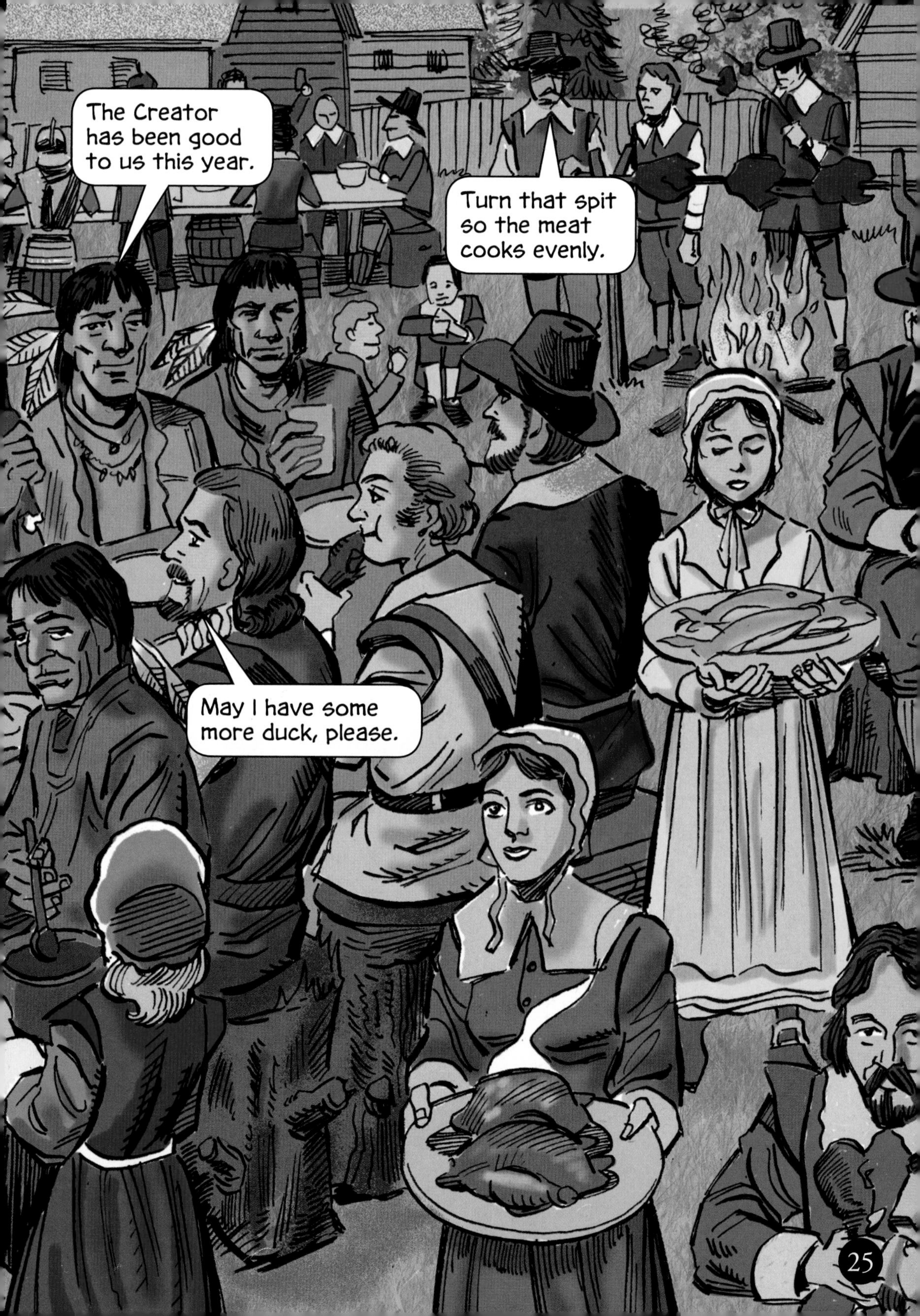
The Creator has been good to us this year.
Turn that spit so the meat cooks evenly.
May I have some more duck, please.

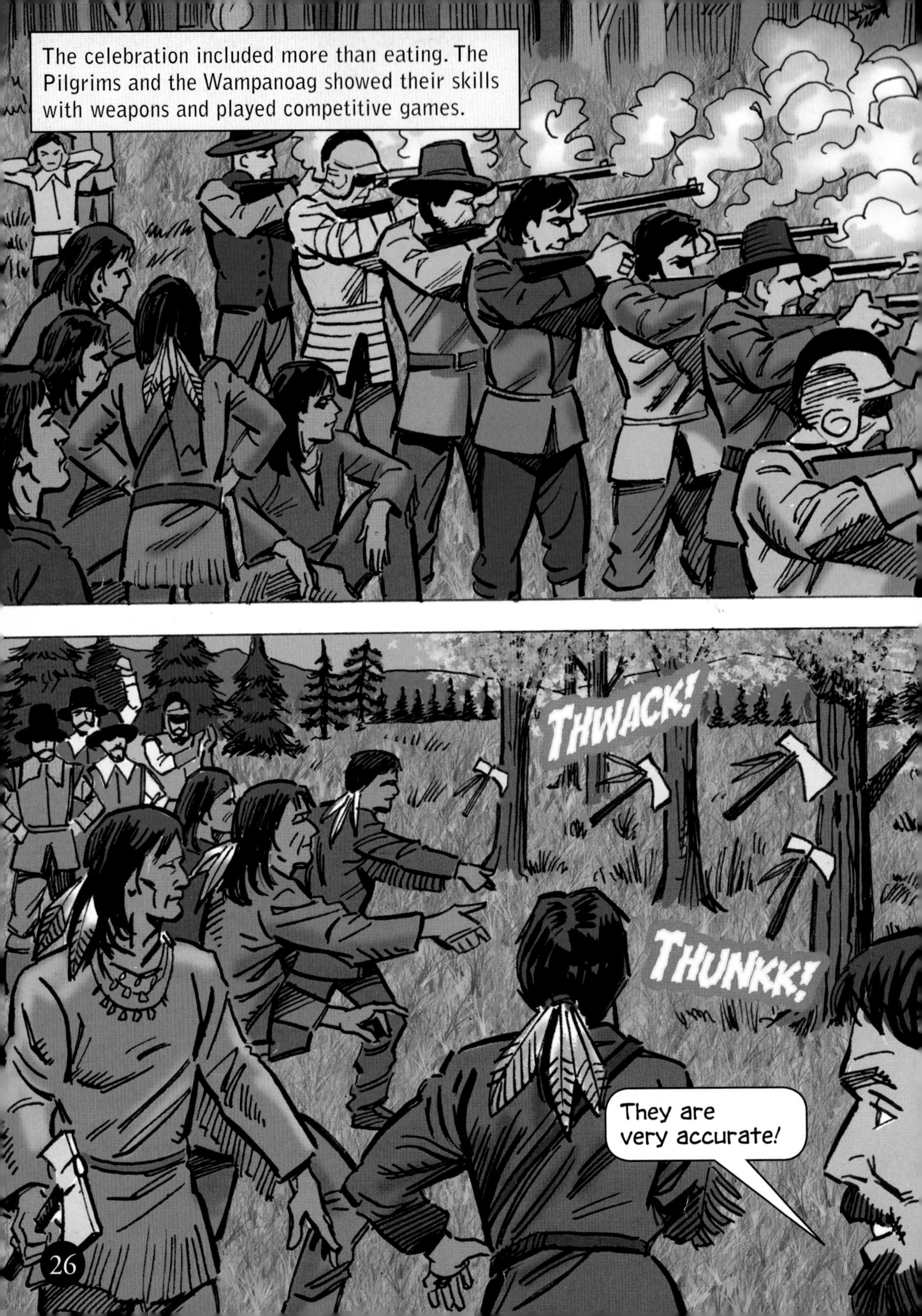
The celebration included more than eating. The Pilgrims and the Wampanoag showed their skills with weapons and played competitive games.
THWACK!
THUNKK!
They are very accurate!

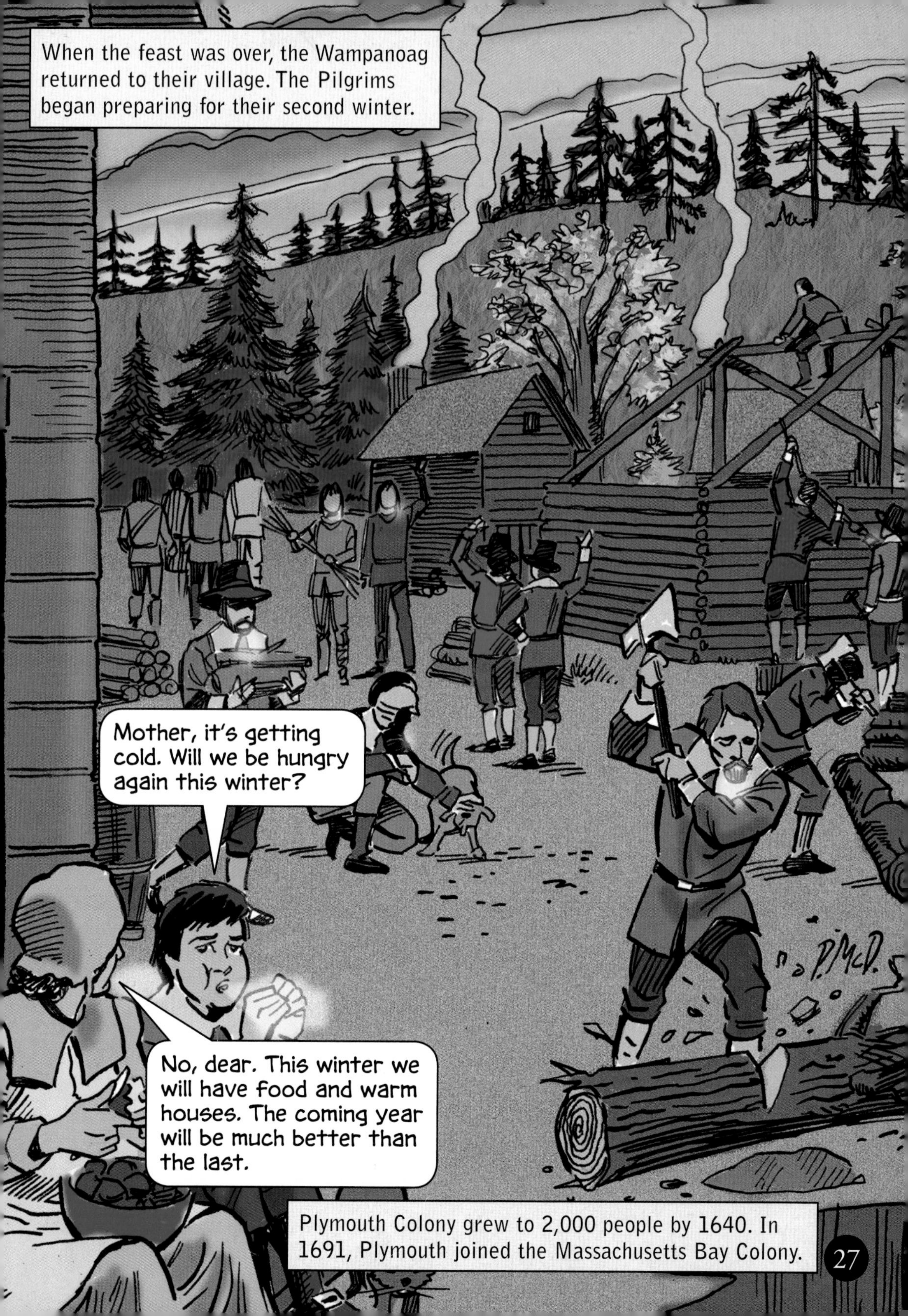
When the feast was over, the Wampanoag returned to their village. The Pilgrims began preparing for their second winter.
Mother, it's getting cold. Will we be hungry again this winter?
No, dear. This winter we will have food and warm houses. The coming year will be much better than the last.
Plymouth Colony grew to 2,000 people by 1640. In 1691, Plymouth joined the Massachusetts Bay Colony.

MORE ABOUT THE Pilgrims AND THE First Thanksgiving

 The people we know as Pilgrims had separated from the Church of England. They were called Separatists. Being a Separatist was against the law in England.

 The Separatists of Plymouth called themselves "Saints." When William Bradford wrote a book about the colony years later, he called them Pilgrims because they traveled a long way for religious freedom.

 Giving thanks was a central part of life for American Indians. They had held thanksgiving feasts for hundreds of years before the Pilgrims arrived.

 The Pilgrims called their first autumn festival the Harvest Feast. To them, a day of thanksgiving meant a day of prayer, with no eating at all.

 Squanto stayed with the Pilgrims until he died of an illness in 1622.

 The peace treaty between Governor Carver and Chief Massasoit lasted for more than 50 years.

Soon after the Pilgrims came to Massachusetts, people called Puritans moved there from England. Their religious beliefs were similar to the Pilgrims' beliefs. But the Puritans stole the Indians' land and tried to force their way of life on them. In 1675, Massasoit's son, Philip, went to war against all the white settlers. In 1676, the white settlers defeated the local Indians and took their land.

 In 1863, President Abraham Lincoln declared the last Thursday in November as Thanksgiving Day. In 1941, President Franklin D. Roosevelt changed the date to the fourth Thursday in November.

 The food enjoyed at the Pilgrims' Harvest Feast was not what most Americans eat when celebrating Thanksgiving. The Pilgrims' meal included deer, fish, and other seafood. If they had turkey at all, it was wild turkey. Potatoes, cranberry sauce, and pumpkin pie were not served at all.

Glossary

Pilgrim (PIL-gruhm)—one of the English Separatists or other colonists who settled in North America in 1620

Separatist (SEP-uh-rah-tist)—one of a group of British people who wanted to practice religion separately from the Church of England

translate (TRANS-late)—to change one language into a different one; Squanto could speak both English and Wampanoag, so he translated for the Pilgrims.

treaty (TREE-tee)—an agreement between two groups of people to be peaceful

Internet Sites

FactHound offers a safe, fun way to find Internet sites related to this book. All of the sites on FactHound have been researched by our staff.

Here's how:
1. Visit *www.facthound.com*
2. Choose your grade level.
3. Type in this book ID **0736854924** for age-appropriate sites. You may also browse subjects by clicking on letters, or by clicking on pictures and words.
4. Click on the **Fetch It** button.

FactHound will fetch the best sites for you!

Read More

Davis, Kenneth C. *Don't Know Much About the Pilgrims.*
New York: HarperCollins, 2002.

Grace, Catherine O'Neill, and Margaret M. Bruchac with
Plimoth Plantation. *1621: A New Look at Thanksgiving.*
Washington, D.C.: National Geographic Society, 2001.

Plimoth Plantation. *Mayflower 1620: A New Look at a
Pilgrim Voyage.* Washington, D.C.: National Geographic
Society, 2003.

Santella, Andrew. *The Plymouth Colony.* We the People.
Minneapolis: Compass Point Books, 2001.

Bradford, William. *Of Plymouth Plantation: 1620–1647.*
New York: Modern Library, 1981.

Bradford, William, and Edward Winslow. *Mourt's Relation
or Journal of the Plantation at Plymouth.* New York: Garrett
Press, 1969.

Deetz, James, and Patricia Scott Deetz. *The Times of Their
Lives: Life, Love, and Death in Plymouth Colony.* New York:
W.H. Freeman, 2000.

Winslow, Edward. *Good Newes from New England.*
Bedford, Mass.: Applewood Books, 1996.

Index